GALA!

ARTS FOR THE AGING, INC. (AFTA)
ELEVENTH ANNIVERSARY GALA

Photo by Didi Cutler

Artwork inspired by Joan Miró.
Created in AFTA workshop led by Laura Huff
at Madison Adult Day Health Care Center.

Under the Gracious Patronage of
H.E. THE AMBASSADOR OF SPAIN AND MRS. OYARZABAL

The Benefit Committee of

ARTS FOR THE AGING, INC. (AFTA)

Invites you to a Buffet Reception

Spanish Specialties

Wednesday, October 6, 1999
6:30-9:00 p.m.

The Residence of the Spanish Ambassador
2801 16th Street, NW
Washington, DC 20009

LIVE AUCTION - SILENT AUCTION
Auctioneer: Robert Aubrey Davis

International Wine Tasting

Cuvee Grand Brut for the Evening Donated by
Perrier-Jouet, Epernay, France

Door Prizes   Guest List at Door
Art Exhibit by AFTA Senior Participants   Valet Parking

GALA!

The Special Event Planner for Professionals and Volunteers

By **Patti Coons**

with **Lois M. Baron**

CAPITAL
BOOKS, INC.
Sterling, Virginia

Capital Books Inc.
P.O. Box 605
Herndon, Virginia 20172-0605

ISBN 1-892123-13-4

Library of Congress Cataloging-in-Publication Data

Coons, Patricia.
    Gala! : the special event planner for professionals and volunteers / by Patricia Coons with Lois M. Baron
         p. cm.
    ISBN 1-892123-13-4 (pbk. : alk. paper)
    1. Special events—Planning. 2. Special events—Management.
  I. Baron. Lois M. II. Title.
GT3405.C66 1999
394.3′068—dc21   99-38962
                                              CIP

Designed by Pen & Palette Unlimited

Printed in the United States of America on acid-free paper that meets the American National Standards Institute Z39-48 Standard.

First Edition

10 9 8 7 6 5 4 3 2 1

Contents

Preface

This book is an all-in-one, step-by-step guide to turning a fund-raising wish into a successful event or for launching an effective fund-raising campaign through a series of events. It teaches you the tried-and-true steps and procedures for pulling it all together—regardless of how large or how small the event is you are staging. You will learn how to put together an informal group of advisors to be your mentors along the way (this book serves much the same function), then how to select the right people for a topnotch event team, how to pick a charity event that fits the cause, and how to find sponsors, contact and involve the media, conduct public seminars, design invitations, raise money, and "wrap up" with a careful analysis of what was good and what could be improved for the next event. In short, you will learn how to plan an event that makes money for your cause and brings quality attention to the group that staged it— your business or nonprofit organization.

I've put all my best experience and ideas into *Gala!* from the hundreds of fundraising events and campaigns I've put on over the years and from the most creative and successful in my friends' and colleagues' portfolios. All of us—volunteers and professionals—need new ideas and strategies for our next big event, so if you have any thoughts, suggestions, or experiences that you would like to share, please send them to me. Your ideas might be in the next edition of this book. Write to me at Capital Books, 22883 Quicksilver Drive, Sterling, Virginia 20166.

Before we begin let me offer thanks to my agent, Rue Judd, my editor, Lois M. Baron, and my publisher, Kathleen Hughes, for their enthusiasm about this book and recognition of its value. They are experienced event planners themselves. And, special appreciation to my parents for all their encouragement and support and belief in me through the years. My best wishes to you, my readers, who make things happen.

Patti Coons

## Chapter 1

How to Use This Book

Very few of us have not been involved in some kind of charity fund-raiser. After all, volunteerism is vital to all nonprofit organizations. Most receive little or no government funds. They are sustained through the efforts of people like you.

Now you have been selected to chair the big fund-raiser or to serve on the event team. It's a huge job, one that may occupy much of your time for many months ahead. And, it's one you are determined will bring many dollars into the coffers of your cause *and* bring credit to your organization. How do you get started?

Welcome to the wonderful world of staging fund-raising events! This book will guide you, step by step, in planning and executing an event that will accomplish all your goals—whether it is a black tie dinner that attracts glittering Hollywood stars and national attention to cystic fibrosis, a political barbecue for your favorite candidate, a charity walk-a-thon, a celebrity speech to honor an award-winner, a school auction whose proceeds will buy new library books, a statewide drive to fund counseling for abused children, or the grand opening event for your new business the funds from which will be donated to cancer research. This handy check-listed guide will show you how. And, it can all be fun, if you follow these guidelines.

The Benefits

For any organization—from a civic group to a school to a corporation—a spectacular fund-raising event has two dividends. It benefits the cause and it boosts your community's awareness about your organization.

Gala! will help you meet your mark, right from the beginning. Sometimes an event makes a splash *because* it is something new and different, but then support dwindles. *Gala!* can help you keep your organization's efforts vibrant and effective by helping you pinpoint what you can do better every year.

 **Tip**

If you are launching a big fund-raising campaign for a charity or a cause, the inaugural event sometimes harvests more community awareness and knowledge than dollars. Don't be disappointed. Use the goodwill and name recognition to make the second special event more financially successful.

Learn Your Community's Big Issues

Knowing your community's interests and issues will help you choose an event that your community will enjoy and look forward to supporting year after year. This knowledge will help you put together a smooth-running, effective event team. And it will help you as you go out into the community looking for support from individuals and businesses, because you'll be better able to contact people likely to support your cause.

 **Tip**

Before selecting a charity to support or launching a campaign, learn your community's interests and issues and meet the people involved in community service and fund-raising.

Find a Mentor and Form an Informal "Team" of Advisors

There may be times when you are put in charge of an event without having the benefit of experience in the particular group or community. Perhaps you've just moved into town. Maybe you decided to volunteer for a big job because you figured it would be like learning to swim—you throw yourself in and either sink or swim. Maybe someone else volunteered you! If you find yourself in such a situation, start by finding someone who has the experience and knowledge you lack, and ask for advice. That person might be someone who held your position last year, someone who has worked on committees for many years, or someone with professional fund-raising experience.

Do some research. If you have a mentor to help you out, terrific. First, assemble a list of everyone you believe would want to be involved. Call each one. When someone can't help you, ask for suggestions of others who might. It's essential to build this team of advisors. And remember: If you believe in the cause, your enthusiasm will be contagious.

 **Tip**

You are the team leader and your enthusiasm for the cause and the event must be real. It's what helps the rest of the team "catch fire." Your enthusiasm will be contagious!

Gala! will be your first stop for information. And it will keep you securely on the right track.

ZOOBILATION '86

Welcome to
Zoobilation '86

L.S. Ayres
September 27, 1986

6:30   Cocktails and Hors d'oeuvres, First Floor North

8:00   Dinner, Eighth Floor Tea Room

9:00   Men's Collections '86

        Awards Presentation Honoring: Jeffrey Banks,
        Jhane Barnes, Andrew Fezza, Henry Grethel,
        Robert Lighton, Robert Stock

9:30   Meet the Designers, First Floor Men's Store

        Animals on Parade

9:30   Dancing, First Floor North

        Photographs with Animals

        Music:

        Drums of Africa
        Al Cobine Orchestra
        Sugar and Spice

## Chapter 2

Selecting the Event

When you begin to consider what kind of an event your team will put on, keep two things in mind:

- You want to involve as many people as possible.
- You want to attract as much media coverage as possible.

Your responsibility is to create and maintain the community's interest in your cause. In doing so, your organization's visibility and credibility will rise.

From the very start, involve the press in your event and fund-raising endeavors. This is vital because the press has the power to affect the success of your project. And, include all the press—daily and weekly newspapers, magazines, and radio and television, both broadcast and cable. Every event will benefit from being announced in the press. Every event will gain stature in the public's mind by being covered by the press.

Selecting a Cause

Many types of organizations raise money. Auxiliaries or supporters of nonprofit organizations, such as Friends of the Zoo, libraries, PTAs, and hospital guilds raise money regularly. Companies, large and small, often support charities as a way of "giving back" to the community. Philanthropic groups and civic organizations, such as the Shriners, the Daughters of the American Revolution, the League of Women Voters, and the Lions Club, fund causes they believe in.

Pick a cause that fits in with the characteristics and goals of your organization and the community you hope to involve. If your group is made up of teenagers, for example, a fund-raising effort focusing on buying books for a homeless shelter will galvanize their enthusiasm. If your business is in an historic building, support the local historic preservation society with your event. If your organization is all women, consider charities that benefit women and families. The charity you select should always interest your core committee and the members of your larger group. Otherwise their enthusiasm will not be there from the beginning. When your committee meets, its members will know it is to work for one cause you all believe in.

 **Tip**

Win their hearts, and their wallets will open.

Reach a Consensus of Your Committee

As you meet as a committee, each of you probably has a project dear to your heart. One member's father might have received an organ transplant, so that person would like to raise money for the Organ Transplant Association, while another might be a breast cancer survivor. One PTA meeting in an elementary school had to determine whether its auction should raise money for a pond that would teach students about aquatic ecosystems or for classroom computers. Each project had proponents, but in the end, they settled on one—and worked as a united group to reach that goal.

Some give-and-take should be involved. As in, "I'll work on your cause this year if you work on my cause in the future." People will work harder on issues they feel strongly about, so it's important to reach a consensus about the cause. Take a poll of your members to find out what they want to support.

Also, as you select a charity, keep in mind that people like to donate for a specific reason. It's easier to convince people to reach for their wallets when they believe in the cause. On a national level, if you're raising money for a particular organization, people want to know what the organization does with the funds. People know and trust organizations like the American Red Cross, the American Heart Association, and United Way because they know the focus of these charities.

The Event Should Fit the Cause

Many nonprofit organizations must raise funds just to support themselves. In recent years, the women's committee of the National Symphony Orchestra in Washington, D.C., for example, has donated the proceeds from its annual Show House to the orchestra's operating budget. Public radio and television stations conduct fund-raising campaigns regularly. PTAs and booster clubs are other examples of organizations that have clearly defined missions. These organizations have a cause; they need to choose the kind of event that will highlight their mission, and, even more importantly, generate the funds they need to survive. And, if your cause is not well known, it may be your first job to define what it is and who benefits from it. An event can do that for you!

With a charity selected, you must decide what type of event you want: a one-shot fund-raiser or several coordinated events over an extended time to reach an overall goal. The possibilities are truly endless. You may focus on raising money, food, clothing, or home improvements for the needy. The only limit is your imagination!

Here is a very short list of the kinds of events you may hold:

- Coffee – A relatively simple way to entertain a large group of prospective voters for a political candidate with coffee and light refreshments in someone's home or a hotel restaurant or meeting room.

- Reception – A more elaborate way to entertain prospective donors or contributors and to introduce a candidate or representatives of a cause, particularly a celebrity who supports it. Receptions are usually held in a large public room, club, or sizable private home. Drinks and hors d'oeuvres are served as refreshments.

- Luncheon – A sit-down or buffet occasion appropriate as an annual fund-raising event because it offers an elegant lunch and accompanying entertainment such as a speaker or a fashion show.

- Dinner or formal gala – Often a much more formal event, which because it is perceived as something really special (elegant menu, creative theme, elaborate flowers and decorations, high-powered speakers and entertainment, often dancing and evening dress) can command a high price-per-person contribution.

- Afternoon tea – An increasingly popular and elegant way to entertain and raise funds for a cause without the elaborate food and expense of a luncheon or dinner.

- Art show or auction – A labor-intensive but very effective event for raising large amounts of money for a cause; needs a very energetic and capable committee to amass and sell a wide range of art or contributed goods in one or many categories. Featuring the art of one well-known artist can also be very lucrative for your charity.

- Cocktail lecture – Less work since only one entertainment (the lecture) is offered, and a good event for reaching a large group of people interested in your cause. If an author is speaking, you can also sell his or her book for a portion of the proceeds.

- Craft workshop, how-to seminar – From flower arranging, to financial planning, bead stringing, anything, this is an excellent community or club event.

- Community garage sale – An effective money-maker if you have a large local group interested in one cause and willing to donate items, time, and their proceeds.

- Sports event – From a celebrity golf or tennis exhibition or tournament to a Little League championship, this is a very entertaining way to raise funds for a cause.

- Home or garden tour – A great way to feature a community cause by putting it on display; requires a lot of volunteers to open their homes or gardens and many more to act as hosts and hostesses.

- Decorator show house – This kind of major fundraiser involves a cast of thousands of volunteers plus plenty of eager interior designers and an architecturally important local house that is for sale and in need of "redoing."

- Christmas decorations competition or holiday greens sale – A seasonal approach to fund-raising allows the holiday spirit to stimulate the contributions.

- Marathon event (walk-a-thon, swim-a-thon, dance-a-thon, etc.) – From the Boston Marathon to a local walk-a-thon for the community food bank, this kind of event requires participating individuals who find their own sponsors, sponsors for the event itself, and many volunteers but can be an effective and healthy way to raise big money, especially for health-related causes.

- Raffle – Be sure to check with state officials about laws governing raffles in your state; there are no laws about drawings, but if you sell raffle tickets, that's a horse of a different color.

- Celebrity roast – See dinner or gala event above. The same conditions apply but a true celebrity will really bring in the crowds for your cause—and often at a high ticket price.

- Bazaar – A time-honored way to pool the resources of an organization or community and have fun raising money.

- Concert – Music and musicians provide the entertainment; you and your committee provide the venue, promotion, and on-site orchestration.

- Phantom event – This is an incredible way NOT to stage an event and people simply send in donations. Your cause has to be very inspirational for it to work, however.

Use your imagination! There are millions of ideas for events. Your goal is to stage an event that highlights your cause, entertains your contributors, and is doable by your committee or staff within your budget.

The Event Should Fit Your Organization

If you are working on a yearlong, national campaign, you should do as many events as is feasible for your organization. If yours is a national company or organization, you can encourage people across the country to try many approaches to reach their local or regional goals.

The kind of charity event you put on depends on such factors as these:

- Size of your organization
- Community standards and expectations

- How much money, goods, or service you want to contribute to your cause

The Size of Your Organization

It is possible for mighty oaks to come from little acorns, but keep in mind that the larger your event is, the more work there is to be done. Choose events that don't overtax yourself, your staff, your resources, and your committee people to the point where no one can muster the energy to work on any other project during the year, and everyone is too tired to work on your event next year. Proper planning will spread the responsibilities and yield happy participation.

Community Standards and Expectations

Every community has a favorite way to make money or generate goods, services, or publicity for charitable causes. In some areas, a yard or tag sale is a standard way to raise money. In others, you can organize a raffle to sell a wonderful quilt, or even feature a Lexus. Every month in the nation's capital, the city magazine carries a long listing of philanthropic galas; in a small rural community in the Midwest, perhaps no organization has ever staged a black tie ball. While you can generate excitement by trying something new, be prepared to overcome people's reluctance about new ventures. It's important to gear your event to the local community—which you know best!

Establish How Much You Want to Raise

It's simple mathematics that a $500-a-plate dinner will produce more money faster than a bake sale—or even a series of bake sales. But, remember: Any event that raises any money for a good cause is a success. Whatever amount you raise is more than the organization would have had if you had not done anything at all, right? On the other hand, why settle for the minimum?

 **Tip**

Set a challenging but realistic goal for your campaign. With a definite goal in sight, your committee has a focus for their campaign and their energy.

Setting a fund-raising goal helps you measure your progress from year to year. If you are launching a new effort—one that your company or organization hasn't undertaken before—you will build year after year, learning from each success and short-fall. If you are in charge of a well-established function, choose a goal that makes you stretch; you don't want to get compla-cent as you put on an event year after year. Find a balance between being ambitious and being realistic in how much you can generate and in the approach you take.

 **Tip**

Determine the per-person ticket price for your event based on estimated per-person costs for staging it.

Your fund-raising goal must also consider how much it will cost to stage the event, attendance expected, and the price you charge. Estimate costs, then set a per-person ticket price that will help you reach your goal after deducting expenses. If you overdecorate or have food that is too luxurious, the money you raise might end up going for expenses, a disheartening end to all your hard work. Set a ticket price that gives the margin needed to reach your goal.

Defining Your Goals

Keep in mind that your goals in planning an event include the following:

- Community involvement
- Leveraging a cause's image
- Building your reputation in the community
- Community outreach
- Benefiting people
- Raising funds
- Raising donations in kind

Once you have chosen your cause and your event, you're ready to move on to the next step, selecting your event team.

Mrs. Melvin Simon and
The Family Support Center Auxiliary
cordially invite you to

A Mystical Night
at the Taj Mahal

on behalf of the
Family Support
Child Crisis Center

Featuring Peter Duchin and his Orchestra

Celebrity Guests

on March 16, 1993 in the
850 Ballroom of the
Indiana Convention Center

6:30–7:30 Open Bar
8:30 Dinner/Dancing
8:30 Music for Dancing

Costume or Black Tie

Creative Chairman - Mrs. Pat Verandah
Co-Chairman - Mrs. Ray Etteldorf

Reservations
Chairman - Mrs. Melvin Simon
Co-Chairman - Mrs. Pat Verandah

Table Decorations
Chairman - Mrs. Melvin Hallbrook
Co-Chairman - Mrs. Pat Feldmann

Program
Chairman - Mrs. Melvin Hallbrook
Co-Chairman - Mrs. Norma Shapiro
Mrs. G.

## Chapter 3

Forming Your Event Team

Your group's event team should consist of enthusiastic, organized, active individuals. Ideally, it will contain people who have been actively involved in the community. In addition to people from your organization, ask key figures from your community's business, government, and local media to join your team. Your event team is the backbone of your charity event. First will come a core group, and then people will be added as time goes by.

 **Tip**

> The makeup of the event team is crucial. Be sure to include responsible yet creative people who have the time to attend committee meetings and are not constantly traveling or dividing their time between more than one home. Each member should have a special talent to offer to the group and not just be a "big name" in the community.

The core group should comprise the following positions:

- Event Chairperson
- Charity Liaison Chair
- Public Relations Chair
- Mailing List Chair
- Donation/Sponsors Chair
- Telephone Solicitation Chair
- Decorating Chair
- Arrangements/Logistics Chair
- Food & Drink Chair
- Invitation & Program Chair
- Reservation Chair
- Volunteer Chair (if applicable)
- Entertainment Chair
- Optional Auction Chair (silent or auctioneer)
- Clean-up Chair

 **Tip**

Each committee chair should keep a notebook detailing deadlines, action items, who is responsible for each, and tasks accomplished. Copies of contracts, bids, and invoices all go into this notebook to provide an organized account of the committee's work—invaluable for record-keeping and planning next year's event.

Committees for Each Chairperson

Every chairperson should have a committee if there is enough work to warrant it. The more people on a committee, the lighter the load for everyone! Try to find experienced people who have worked on this event in previous years or on other fund-raisers—but reach out to new people as well.

Encourage newcomers to serve or participate in charitable causes. Reach out to people in different age groups, vocations, and neighborhoods. It's never too early to teach youngsters the value of helping others, and many retirees would be happy to be serving a worthy cause.

College and high school students are a rich source of energy and enthusiasm, if the event is appropriate for that age group. Students provide extra hands for you, while charity fund-raisers provide wonderful training for paying jobs in the "real world." Try approaching clubs, fraternities, and sororities for volunteers; it can definitely pay off for everyone.

One way to find people who share your interests is to advertise a meeting—in the newspaper, on television, or in local bulletins and newsletters. There's always some worthy person searching for a worthy cause.

Event Chairperson

 **Tip**

> A good chairperson is energetic, conscientious, organized, responsible, has good contacts, and likes and manages people well.

This person

- Acts as the team leader for the event.
- Schedules event team core committee meetings.
- Follows up with team members on progress made and overall coordination of efforts and activities involved with putting on an event.

- Makes sure that everything is done, whether this means delegating to a responsible person or stepping in to fill a gap.

The truth is, when you're selecting a chair or thinking about volunteering as chair, other factors are at play as well. A good chair will be

- Well liked and respected.
- Noncontroversial.
- Able to work with many different personalities. (Volunteers can't be fired.)
- Able to quash his or her own ego for the good of the event.
- Well known in the community that the event will involve.
- Able to delegate. Even though it's true that 20 percent of the people do 80 percent of the work, if you do all the work, you'll damage something—your health, your relationship with your family, or your willingness to work on an event after this one event is over.
- Willing to shoulder the responsibility when someone doesn't follow through.
- Willing to ask for help—both for information and advice. You can always learn from others and get somebody to help you.
- Receptive to ideas from others.

 **Tip**

> The event chairperson is above all a leader who knows how to keep the wheels rolling smoothly.

The chair should also

- Know who in the community are good workers and who has the time to contribute. It might be tempting to choose friends as committee chairs, but if you know in your heart of hearts that a friend is not a diligent worker, resist the temptation.

- Know key players in the community. It can be the difference between netting $10,000 for the fund-raiser and netting $50,000.

- Put aside personal feelings to do what's best for the charity and best for the event.

- Be respected in the community.

- Be able to convey a sense of warmth to everyone with whom he or she works.

 **Tip**

> If the event chairperson doesn't know what he or she is doing, the other committee chairs will begin to doubt their abilities too. Feelings can get hurt, people can become angry, and friendships can be destroyed. With all this turmoil, your event will not reach its goals.

Although different people are in charge of different aspects of the fund-raising event, the chair is ultimately responsible for it all. On the day of the event, he or she should run through a master list, called a staging guide by professional event planners, with the arrangements/logistics chair.

Event Checklist

A suggested listing of items to check for successful event planning includes the following:

- ❏ Menu selection with guarantees for how many will attend
- ❏ Number at head table, with a diagram of seating
- ❏ Number at other tables
- ❏ Place cards
- ❏ Diagram of room setup
- ❏ Name tags (make sure extras and pens are available)
- ❏ Decorations
- ❏ Music
- ❏ Spokesperson
- ❏ Deadline for having room set up
- ❏ Seating
- ❏ Audiovisual needs
- ❏ Lighting
- ❏ Room temperature
- ❏ Programs
- ❏ Party favors

 **Tip**

The event chairperson is much more effective if he or she really believes in the cause. His or her enthusiasm will give the other committee members strength.

Recheck before Event

- ❏ Room open and staffed
- ❏ Seating style as ordered
- ❏ Public address (PA) system working

❑ Staging set up as ordered
❑ Lighting
❑ Cooling/heating system operating
❑ Piped-in music (make sure you have access to and control of any piped-in music)

Charity Liaison Chair

- Acts as a liaison between the event team and the charity's headquarters.

- Obtains information and materials from the charity's headquarters as the event is developed.

- Lines up a charity spokesperson to publicize the event and speak at it.

- Relays information gleaned from the national charity headquarters with the other chair people.

- Encourages a representative of the charity to attend every event team meeting.

Your first order of business is to

❑ Contact the charity's public relations or marketing department and ask what material the department can provide you. Often the charity will have brochures, videos, slide presentations, and fact sheets.
❑ If you receive a video, ask for a written script of the tape.
❑ If the charity office sends a slide presentation, ask that the slides be identified so that you can make sure they're in the right order. Ask for a script with notations as to where each slide should be used.

❑ If there is not a slide presentation, but the charity does have slides, ask that the contents of each slide be identified so you can prepare your own show.

 **Tip**

Often a national charity already has a celebrity associated with its cause. Work with the headquarters to place your event on the spokesperson's calendar of appearances so he or she can promote it and lend the support of his or her friends and colleagues.

The liaison chair should get to know the charity's board of directors or advisory board, perhaps by taking them to lunch or dinner. Fostering friendships among board members makes it easier to ask the charity how to do something—and easier to understand how the charity works. It also gives you the opportunity to introduce your group to these often influential people.

Public Relations Chair

- Contacts the media and establishes personal relationships with key figures.
- Prepares "fast fact" sheet.
- Generates press releases.
- Prepares schedule for distribution of press releases.
- Invites press contacts to attend the function.
- Provides media information to the mailing list chairperson.

See the chapter on media relations for a full explanation of the work involved with heading up this committee. This person must be willing to follow up, follow up, follow up!

Mailing List Chair

 **Tip**

> One way to expand the mailing list quickly is to require each member on the mailing committee or the entire event team to contribute 30 to 50 names. The mailing committee should organize these names into the mailing list, eliminating duplications, of course.

- Compiles the contact mailing list. Obtains additions to the list from other committee members and from the contacts made by other committee chairs. Works closely with other committee chairs to incorporate all the lists supplied by the national or regional charity and those from everyone on the committee.
- Checks for duplicates after the mailing list has been compiled.
- Sees that invitation envelopes are addressed by hand if possible.
- Buys and affixes stamps. Do not use a postal meter!
- Writes (or has printed) and encloses a short personal note from the committee chair or appropriate member with each invitation. It means more to have a small personalized card with the invitation saying "Hope you will join us at our event," signed by the chair or a friend.

The best person for this very important job is someone who

- Has been involved in fund-raising for several years.
- Is familiar with the community and outside mailing lists.

Tip

> Invitations addressed by hand are more appealing. This personal touch gives warmth and a note of elegance to the invitation, and makes guests feel more important.

If possible, address invitations by hand. Nothing on labels or printed by a computer. If your event is huge, make sure you have a big committee to handle this task. You can make the addressing lighter and fun: Serve a light lunch for the committee to write notes and address envelopes all on one day.

If money is no object, you can hire a calligrapher. Make sure you allot enough time for the calligrapher to do his or her work and still get the invitations out on time. Remember to ask if the calligrapher will donate all or part of his or her services—and check to see if a committee member has this skill. Computer software programs are now available to print envelopes with a calligraphy-type script.

If you can't afford to pay a professional to address all the invitations, consider doing just your "A-list" donors. It's also possible to hand-deliver these invitations in festive and creative ways, such as tying a balloon to each envelope and personally delivering the invitations.

Tip

> Mail invitations at least a month ahead to allow people time to place the event on their social calendars—especially during the busy seasons of the year.

Exactly how far in advance you mail the invitations depends on how much time you have allotted to putting your event together. For very elaborate events, you might mail invitations a couple of months ahead. Usually three or four weeks before is adequate.

Donation/Sponsors Chair

- Gets as many goods and services as possible donated for the staging of the event.
- Requests donations from individuals and business donors.
- Notifies the public relations chair of all the sponsors that should be recognized in press releases.
- Makes sure donations are acknowledged in the printed program.
- Is efficient.

In the volunteer world, rarely does a fund-raising project get allotted a budget from the outset. But costs can be determined and are very helpful when arranging for underwriting. The name of the game is "See what you can get donated." Ideally, donations will cover the goods and services needed to stage the fund-raising event—for example, food, decorations, location, printing, party favors. The person in this position works closely with the charity chairperson to find possible donors and casts a wide net in asking people to be on the donation committee.

 **Tip**

Vendors know that a fund-raising event is a great place to "advertise" their services to an important audience. Never hesitate to ask them to donate their services. It's free advertising for them.

If you can place on the committee people who have an "in" with services that you need, you can often get a price break, if not a full donation. Caterers usually give a tremendous discount and even donate food. Printers can be very generous for the simple addition of a line saying "Courtesy of . . ." on the printed program. Sometimes businesses want to be anonymous, however, so that they will not be flooded with requests for donations.

Telephone Solicitation Chair

- Organizes the follow-up phone contact to targeted supporters. This phone calling makes sure that invitations have been received and are considered. A large committee is important to share the workload.

- Works closely with the people mailing the invitations. A week after invitations are dropped into the postal system, phones should begin ringing.

- Makes sure top donors are contacted by committee members who know them, for the best response. If the invitees can't attend, they should be asked if they will support a corporate table or make a donation.

- Three weeks before the event, invitees should be called again if no response has been forthcoming.

- After the event, whether they attended or donated, prominent invitees should receive a final phone call. If they made a pledge, they should be thanked and reminded to put the event on their calendar for next year. If they didn't come, the caller should say something like, "We're so sorry you weren't able to attend, but we hope you'll put us on your calendar for next year."

- Gives people on this committee specific guidelines and directions to help them in their calls. Ten people is a reasonable number to expect each committee member to call. Try to make sure that no one gets overlapping lists; you don't want two people calling the same invitee.

Tip

Be pleasant, positive, and enthusiastic when calling guests and major contributors. Know how to give accurate but inspiring information about your cause.

Decorating Chair

- Responsible for acquiring and setting up the tables and flowers, and creating the overall ambience. The chair and committee will choose the theme.
- Makes sure the decorations are nonflammable, especially if candles are on the tables.

The charity event is well served if the decorating chair is

- Creative.
- Artistic or has design experience.

A local florist is a good choice for membership on this committee, because a florist will steer you toward good centerpieces at affordable prices. (Consider selling the centerpieces to cover the cost, with any profit being donated to your designated charity.) Other good choices include a local theater set designer, gardeners, or a garden club's award winner. It's possible for the committee to create the event's centerpieces themselves, especially when gardens are in bloom!

- Selects, obtains, and distributes party favors. The decorating chair and the donations chair need to put their heads together with the entertainment chair to find small, attractive, useful items that will coordinate with the event's theme and tone. It would be a shame, for example, to send people home from an elegant black tie evening with lifeless, unappealing gifts in a plain brown paper bag.

- Sometimes the entertainer serves as a natural tie-in to party favors or another part of the event. Elizabeth Taylor has been known to give samples of her signature perfume, "Passion," at promotional events, for example.

- If the speaker for the evening is an author, the party favor could be an autographed volume of the person's book.

Arrangements/Logistics Chair

- Arranges for location.
- Arranges parking, if necessary.
- Coordinates with the decorating and entertainment committees to make sure everything is taken care of in the physical space where the event will be held.
- Makes certain the room is open as necessary for setup and the event.
- Arranges for a committee to help decorate on the day of the event.
- Responsible for room setup, including seating and space for speakers or entertainment.
- Makes sure audiovisual needs are met.
- Rents mobile phones or pagers if event warrants it.
- Is in charge of lighting.
- Is in charge of room temperature.
- Has access to and control of any piped-in music.

Tip

One liter of liquor serves 22 drinks at 1½ ounces per drink, or approximately 7 or 8 people.

One bottle of wine serves 6 drinks at 4 ounces—which means partially filling the glasses. A bottle will yield 5 glasses if you fill glasses more generously.

One gallon of wine serves 33 drinks at 4 ounces each.

Calculate 2 drinks per person for a one-hour cocktail hour, and remember most people forget where they leave their glasses and order a fresh drink. Make sure you have plenty of extra glasses, which, unless your event is extremely informal, should be glass, rather than paper or plastic.

Have on hand: bottled water, club soda, tonic water, soft drinks, fruit juices.

Food & Drink Chair

- Selects caterer and menu within a budget.
- Arranges for liquor license, if required.
- Decides how much food and drink will be needed.
- Finds restaurants, caterers, or people to donate food and drinks.
- Arranges for transportation of food and drink to event location, if necessary.
- Arranges for food and drink service, including the flatware, serving dishes, napkins, and staff, which may be provided by a caterer or hotel food service.
- Arranges a "tasting" party for the committee before the event.

The chair should count on a 5 percent margin of error and guarantee the food service people a smaller number than the number of people who have said they are coming—but make sure that more people can be accommodated if necessary. If 500 say they are coming, the food service staff will set up for 500, but be guaranteed payment for 475 guests. That way you don't end up paying for no-shows. Ask your caterer if it will be difficult to add a table at the last minute if necessary.

- Having several bar locations avoids overcrowding and lines.

Invitation & Program Chair

- Oversees the design and printing of invitations, map, programs, place cards, and so forth. This committee selects an appropriate printer and designs the invitations and any other printed material, making sure that all the pertinent information is included. Pertinent information on the invitation or program includes what type of event it is; when, where, and what time the event will be held; and prices or suggested donations.

- Works with event chairperson to develop "donor categories" so that guests can be recognized for donations that are more than the ticket price—whether or not they attend.

- Makes sure the entire event team proofreads the invitation. The team should go through the copy carefully to make sure all the pertinent information is included. On programs, it's important to make sure all the sponsors who want to be recognized on the program are included and that their names are spelled correctly. Check and double-check. Is someone in your group a professional editor?

- All parties who need to look at the program and invitation should initial them.
- Makes sure the invitations are printed on schedule so they can be addressed and sent out on time.
- Uses live postage (stamps), whenever possible, on the invitations, not metered mail.
- Prepares a program: Have the event team review and proof this text and format.
- Prints the program at the last minute to accommodate additions and changes.

Tip

Wherever possible, include personal notes from committee members in the appropriate invitations. For those invitees you do not know personally, include a generic note from the chair, such as "Hope you will join us—Patti Coons, chair."

Tip

Meet all printer deadlines.

Reservation Chair

- Receives and compiles all responses and moneys sent in answer to the invitations.
- Plans the seating charts and is responsible for the place cards for seating.
- Creates and distributes name tags if they're used. (Do not use name tags at formal events.)

The chair of this committee is best served if he or she

- Identifies people who need particularly good seats—whether they are major donors, whether they belong to the headquarters of the charity you're supporting, and so on. If the chair has any doubts or questions about who should sit with whom, he or she should ask the charity chairperson for guidance.
- Identifies seating for anyone with disabilities.
- Coordinates seating decisions with the charity liaison chair, who will be familiar with the important people to invite from the charity headquarters.
- Has tact.
- Is attentive to detail.
- Coordinates and supervises ushers or greeters.

Volunteer Chair

- Works with other chairs to fill responsibilities with volunteers to free up the other chairs to concentrate on other aspects of their jobs.
- Puts together a volunteer schedule, charting who is responsible for what task.

Entertainment Chair

The entertainment chair organizes any entertainment or music required for the event. If you are working closely with a charity organization, the charity may recommend people who have worked well with other events. It may be that an entertainer is already associated with the particular charity you are supporting.

This chairperson

- Assigns one person to handle the arrival, pickup, transportation, and so forth for any entertainers who are coming in for the event so that there's no miscommunication between committee members.

- Works particularly closely with the decorating and donations chairs.

Optional Auction Chair

If your event will include an auction, this chair (supported by a large and energetic committee)

- Develops and coordinates the silent auction for the event, if one is held.
- Coordinates with the auctioneer, if a live auction is taking place.
- Coordinates the solicitation, pickup, and delivery of donations.
- Prepares a list with descriptions of auction items for the program.
- Designs and prints bid sheets for silent auction.
- Sets up auction tables.
- Schedules when bidding on each table will close (a staggered schedule makes sure the cashier is not overwhelmed).
- Receives auction money at the event.

 **Tip**

Items that receive no bids can be moved to a sale table, where prices will be slashed.

Tip

Tables for the silent auction might be organized by auction items:
— Day Trips and Getaways
— Services and Lessons
— Arts and Treasures
— Food and Restaurants
— Gift Baskets
— Sports or Celebrity Memorabilia

The chairperson of this committee should be someone who is

- In tune with a range of different businesses.
- Understands what constitutes desirable items.
- Forceful in a nice way.
- Never one to hear the word "no"!

Optional Honorary Chair

Usually the position of honorary chair is filled by a notable public official, diplomat, author, or celebrity. Often this person has a relationship to the cause. Sometimes the charity you are affiliating with already has a celebrity spokesperson. This will make your job easier.

You should expect an honorary chair to

- Lend his or her name to your efforts.
- Promote your event(s) when he or she is in public.
- Suggest that his or her friends and acquaintances donate to your event.
- Attend a reception for the top donors.

- Spread the word that he or she is participating in your fund-raiser.

Clean-up Chair

- Understands how much clean-up will be required—whether that means vacuuming up every piece of confetti, stacking the chairs, or just turning off the lights, securing the floor, and leaving it all for the janitor, caterer, or trash removal company.

 **Tip**

The clean-up chair makes certain that the clean-up requirements of the location are met.

## Chapter 4

Establishing Your Event Calendar

You can throw to-gether an event at the last minute, but the rewards for start-ing early are so much greater. You save wear-

Tip

The more you plan in advance, the easier it will be on the committee—and the greater your rewards.

and-tear on yourself and your colleagues. You generate more good "buzz" for your event and better participation and attendance. You cultivate goodwill. And you raise much more money, goods, attention, or services to help the cause you have selected. Aren't those goals worth early organization?

Plan, Plan, Plan

While a bake sale might be organized in a month, for a large event, seven months to a year in advance is not too early to develop your team and your work plan. You can't put on an event like the Indianapolis 500 Ball, which attracts thousands of attendees a year, in a flash. It takes time to organize and sell corporate tables for $10,000, for example. If you are mounting an extensive campaign that will involve several events to raise money and support for a particular cause, you'll use a yearlong calendar.

For one-time or smaller events, a less extensive calendar is needed—but equally essential. Each step in the calendar can be shortened if your event is smaller in scale, but consider each step carefully to see if it could boost the success of your organization's event. You still need to do the activities listed on the calendar, whether you spread them out over a long period of time or must compress them into a shorter one.

You can use and reuse these calendars as you develop your own events and charity campaigns. The schedules show you when to employ each tool—all of which you will learn about in this book—to generate the greatest community participation and press coverage possible.

In the beginning, the core group of committee chairs—the event team—should meet once a month. Make sure you choose energetic, hard-workers for the event team, people who will be around to help. Beginning three months before your big day, the committee should meet twice a month, and a month before your event, you should get together once a week. Each subsidiary committee meets between complete event team get-togethers.

For a Yearlong Campaign or Major Event

When you plan a publicity campaign that will encourage people to take action throughout the year—whether to donate to the United Way or to become a member of a museum guild—you will use a twelve-month calendar. Generally one large event will form the keystone of your campaign, and you will plan for that event on a nine-month schedule.

In addition, you may need to plan some smaller satellite events throughout the year to spark enthusiasm, increase awareness and membership, and generate action and contributions in the community. Both the large event and the smaller ones will need to be carefully coordinated so that your organization is not overtaxed and so that each event can shine. And as soon as your wrap-up meeting is done for the entire year, you'll start immediately on planning for the next year.

Many major events also take a year to plan. For either a yearlong campaign or a major event, groundwork listed in the calendar for Months 1 and 2 need to be completed at least six months before the event.

Month 1

(7 to 10 months before major event)

Month 1 is strictly organizational. You will be busy gathering information and contacts. You will customize this calendar to your specific needs. The larger your event team is, the greater your likelihood for success.

- ❑ Determine what kind of event you would like to hold, such as a luncheon, reception, seminar, cocktail lecture, formal or informal dinner, or a variety of separate events as part of a campaign.
- ❑ Set goals and a budget for your event.
- ❑ Determine timeline needed to accomplish each event.
- ❑ Recruit your event team.
- ❑ Solicit proposals from caterers and other vendors.
- ❑ Determine your target audience and create a mailing list.
- ❑ Contact the headquarters of your charity, if one exists, to learn what help they can provide, such as materials, mailing lists, and advice.
- ❑ Ask that the charity's executive director or a representative attend all your event team meetings.
- ❑ Reserve an event site.

❏ Gather the names, addresses, phone and fax numbers, and e-mail or Web site addresses of helpful local business and community leaders.

❏ Assemble a media contact list. Identify media you wish to target: magazines, newspapers, radio and TV. Check carefully for correct addresses and appropriate contacts.

❏ Establish a Web site. Appoint a knowledgeable person to be in charge of it and to keep the site updated.

Tip

In addition to the "who, what, when, where, and why" details of your event, your Web site can contain a corporate or organization history, a graphic showing the level of donations throughout the campaign, and a list of coming events or deadlines.

Month 2

(At least 6 months before major event)

In Month 2 your event team will meet and you'll assign duties. Be sure you and your committees are well informed about the charity or institution you are supporting, contacts, and ideas for future events.

❏ Refine mailing and invitation lists.

❏ Schedule and plan any seminars you wish to do as part of the fund-raising campaign or event publicity.

❏ Contact local, state, or national organizations to set up announcements or public speaking engagements for presentations about the charity or event you're sponsoring.

❏ Prepare all presentation material that you will give to the boards of any groups you approach for support.

❏ If you are fund-raising for a charity, contact the charity's central office (which may be at the national, state, or city level) to obtain any brochures, slides shows, videos, or other promotional material.

❏ Prepare and send press releases and press kits announcing the event or fund-raiser. Include information about both your organization and the projects or program you're supporting.

❏ Update Web site.

Month 3

(5 months before major event)

This month is a busy one. You'll be checking to make sure that the event team committees are on track.

❏ Refine mailing list, checking that everyone has contributed names of friends and acquaintances and that there are no duplications.

❏ Write and design the invitation. Be sure to include all necessary information and clear directions.

❏ Offer to speak to local organizations such as the Rotary Club, hospital and museum guilds, neighborhood associations, special-interest clubs, and schools. Ask them to support your cause, either financially or with contributions of time or resources.

❏ Sponsor seminars of interest to the public or to civic or hobby associations (e.g., Junior League, garden clubs). The seminar subject doesn't have to be about your event or the cause (the seminar could be about decluttering, a popular subject, but make it clear that your organization is donating proceeds to charity).

❏ Send out press releases before and after you have a speaking engagement or seminar. Include a photo from the speaking engagement with your "after" release.

- ❑ Follow up your network of contacts with information and opportunities for participation.
- ❑ Contact local companies for contributions and sponsorships.
- ❑ Make physical arrangements for the event, such as firming up the location, spokesperson, food, entertainment, and audiovisual needs.
- ❑ Be certain to have adequate parking. Where space is limited, you may want to offer valet parking.
- ❑ Continue contacting active members of the community, interest groups, media, city officials, key community leaders.

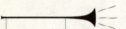 **Tip**

Consider a temporary Web site or e-mail address for publicizing your event. Speeches at clubs, associations, and fraternal organizations have long been an effective way to generate support. You can give a short talk about the cause and the event you're sponsoring, distributing brochures from the charity headquarters along with information about your own organization. Send a press release to local media before the event with a photo of key figures to generate some media coverage of your cause. By getting into the public eye you'll publicize not only your event but also the work of your group, institution, or company in the business community and community service areas.

Month 4

(4 months before major event)

Concentrate on making sure your event team is getting its work done.

- ❑ Conduct public speaking engagements and any seminars.
- ❑ Make sure key officials and active members of the community know about your event.

- ❏ Order invitations. Proof invitations carefully! Have several proofreaders; each should initial the proof.
- ❏ Keep media contacts well informed. Give them detailed information about the date, time, and place.
- ❏ Continue to send out press releases before and after speaking engagements, including a photo of the speaking engagement with the "after" release.
- ❏ Select and order souvenirs.

 **Tip**

Send letters confirming all arrangements with written contracts signed by the chair of the event.

Month 5

(3 months before major event)

Follow up with your event team.

- ❏ Send advance invitations to sponsors and underwriters.
- ❏ Send invitations to prominent people.
- ❏ Continue speaking to special interest groups.
- ❏ If you have a charity spokesperson, follow up to make sure your event is on his or her schedule and that the logistics are worked out.
- ❏ Continue networking with officials and community leaders.
- ❏ Send the appropriate media a press release about the event team itself. Include a photo of the members.
- ❏ Continue to send out press releases before and after public speaking engagements.
- ❏ Update Web site.

❑ Follow up with arrangements for catering, rentals, and other physical details.

❑ Finalize invitation and mailing list.

◀≡ **Tip**

Check spelling of all personal names, and be certain that professional titles are correct.

Month 6

(2 months before the event)

Make sure that your event team is meeting deadlines for their various assignments.

❑ Continue public speaking engagements.

❑ Prepare to mail invitations four to six weeks before your event if it is a massive one (otherwise, wait until three or four weeks in advance).

❑ Schedule a gathering of committee members to address invitations.

❑ Have committee members write personal notes with or on the invitation.

❑ Immediately follow up on the invitations sent to "key" invitees to ask for their commitment to attend your event. (See "Invitation Follow-up Sample Phone Script.")

❑ Follow up event arrangements.

❑ Meet with key officials or community business leaders, such as over lunch, to discuss charity and stimulate more interest and involvement.

❑ Target business and community organizations, key city officials, and interest groups with your event's promotional material and a personal call from a committee member.

❏ Send a press release about the event accompanied by a photo of key people in your organization with the endorsing celebrity, spokesperson, or charity sponsor.

❏ Decide when and how your event will conclude.

❏ Check to see if you need insurance, sales tax application, and liquor licenses.

Month 7

(1 month before the event)

Keep checking up with the event team and go through the final preparation checklist below.

❏ Determine who will be in a receiving line.

❏ Take a key official or community business leader to lunch to discuss your event and stimulate more interest and involvement.

❏ Confirm speaker and entertainment. Arrange for a backup speaker in case an emergency prevents your first choice from appearing.

❏ Have the hotel food service or caterer prepare and present a trial dinner for a small number of committee members.

❏ As invitations are mailed and responses received, follow up with phone calls. By calling, you make sure the invitation was received and that all the information about the event is clear.

❏ Prepare a realistic agenda/schedule for speakers, participants, and entertainment with specific time limits, and confirm with participants.

❏ Prepare a printed program if appropriate.

❏ If you are conducting a yearlong campaign, hold a seminar that the public will want to attend.

❏ Keep in touch with business and community organizations, key city officials, interest groups.

- ❑ Send out press releases and public service announcements about the event, stating location and event goals.
- ❑ Update Web page.
- ❑ Post signs in public places announcing the event (if appropriate).
- ❑ Review assignments with committee for day of the event.
- ❑ Reserve mobile phones or intercom for committee members to keep in touch with each other during the event if logistics warrant it.
- ❑ Be prepared for the unexpected, such as bad weather or speaker cancellation. Have a contingency plan for each, such as rental facilities for a tent.
- ❑ Plan for a medical professional, such as a company nurse, to be on hand for emergencies during the event.

◀≡ Tip

In a receiving line, guests are usually greeted by the event chairperson, a charity representative, and the head of the organization sponsoring the event. At a Habitat for Humanity International fund-raiser, for example, the receiving line would consist of the HFHI president and the national chair.

One Week before the Event

- ❑ Send a final press release to media you are targeting. Include any new noteworthy information, such as celebrities or dignitaries expected to attend.
- ❑ Make follow-up calls to media five days before the event. Keep calling until you have definite commitments from the media to cover the event.
- ❑ Confirm refreshments, audio equipment, seating, rest rooms, first aid, photographer, supplies, flowers, decor, entertainment, and so forth.

❑ Review and update RSVP list daily.

❑ Keep in daily contact with the caterer, for changes in the number of expected guests. Caterers will require you to give a "guarantee" by a specific date. After that date, numbers can only go up.

❑ Finalize the program and have it printed.

❑ Prepare a step-by-step agenda for the big day. Include ALL pertinent information on this staging guide (p. 58).

❑ Conduct a dress rehearsal of the event with core committee members from start to finish. If that is not possible, at least check the sound system.

❑ If possible, have the keynote speaker rehearse. If this is not feasible, make sure that he or she knows what to do from the moment of arrival through departure.

❑ Confirm that your staging guide is realistic: Double-check times and set time limits for speakers, entertainment, participants, and the core committee.

Day of the Event

❑ Be organized so that you can start on time.

❑ Follow the confirmed staging guide.

❑ Allow for extra time, because something will always go wrong.

❑ Provide transportation for any dignitaries and guest speakers who need it.

❑ Distribute confirmed agenda to keynote speakers, participants, and core committee. Make sure they know what to do.

❑ Set up media registration table with press kits.

❑ Display table assignments at the entry.

❑ Be sure greeters or ushers are in place.

❑ Form receiving line.

❑ Circulate as much as you can while still enforcing the agenda—or designate someone to watch the clock for you.

- [ ] Have guests sign in, if appropriate.
- [ ] For last-minute cancellations, fill in no-shows at prominent tables with volunteer staff.
- [ ] End the event at a specific time.
- [ ] Have copies of your guest list available for future uses.

Month 8

(Within 2 weeks after the event)

Focus on the people you have invited and sponsors/donors. Thanking event donors and participants will ensure future participation.

- [ ] Follow up immediately with donors and key event participants.
- [ ] Send a press release highlighting the event's success, goals reached, active participants, and donors. Include photos.
- [ ] Hold event team wrap-up meeting, while details of the event are fresh.

 **Tip**

Send thank-you notes to all active participants, donors, supporters. Call selected guests to thank them for their participation and support.

Month 9

(1 month after the event)

After the event, you can bask in your success—and be certain to have thanked active participants and donors who made it possible! You also need to critique the event and begin planning your next event.

❏ Take care of thank-you notes and calls.
❏ Update Web site.

Month 10

(2 months after the event)

❏ Set up the calendar for a new project.
❏ Update Web site.

Midsized Event

Many events can be pulled off with flair starting two months before you want to hold your event—whether it is to raise donations for a charity, stage a grand opening for a business, promote interest in your gardening club's activities, celebrate the publication of a friend's book, or generate general awareness about an institution or company.

 **Tip**

> Many productive events are heavily networked; that is, "You support my cause and I'll support yours," is the event planner's motto.

Six to Eight Weeks before the Event

❏ Select and invite committee members to a meeting.
❏ Make sure you have everyone's home and office phone and fax numbers, as well as e-mail addresses.
❏ Select date, time, and location.
❏ Determine timeline needed to accomplish each task.
❏ Decide on budget, if needed. Most fund-raisers do not have a budget per se, since they count on donations to take care of their needs, but estimating costs ahead of

time and planning a per-person ticket price based on covering these costs and making a profit will clearly help you plan more effectively and make more from your event.

❏ Draw up a "Responsibility/Status Report" (p. 57).

❏ Determine if you want to set up a Web site for the event, who will be in charge of it, and how frequently it will be updated.

❏ Select and invite speaker(s) or entertainment.

❏ Delegate authority on assignment lists for each committee and know where and what everyone is doing for the event and at the event.

❏ Arrange for menu, photographer, audio equipment, seating, rest rooms, first aid, supplies, decor, entertainment, materials for any presentations or ribbon-cutting (e.g., plaques, ribbons, oversize scissors).

❏ Check to see if you need insurance and any licenses (such as for selling liquor) for the event.

❏ Order invitations.

❏ Select and order souvenirs.

❏ Have a backup for outdoor events in case of inclement weather, such as a tent rental or an alternate place.

❏ Begin compiling a guest list, which will include media, local dignitaries, and celebrities as well as area businesspeople and the public, friends, or potential customers, depending on the nature of your event.

❏ Meet with chairs of other charities, civic groups, and political organizations for their advice on the local community. Compare notes about what worked well and what didn't.

❏ Consider parking needs and make sure you have enough spaces to accommodate the number of expected guests. For a more formal event, or where space is limited, you may want to offer valet parking.

❏ Compile a notebook with all your information (i.e., to-do lists, phone numbers of suppliers, correspondence) for easy reference.

Four Weeks before the Event

❏ Be prepared for the unexpected. For example: Have a backup for your keynote speaker.

❏ Write a newsworthy press release.

❏ Prepare and send out to media a press kit that includes the press release, history of the company or organization sponsoring the event, photographs, and brochures. Make sure you have extra kits to distribute at the event.

❏ Follow up on pre-event publicity with a new press release and follow-up calls to media.

❏ Post signs in public places announcing the event (if open to the public).

❏ Review assignments with committee for day of the event.

❏ Reserve walkie-talkies for committee to keep in touch with each other during the event if logistics warrant it.

❏ Mail invitations to all guests with phone numbers to RSVP and explicit directions.

❏ Plan for a medical professional, such as a company nurse, to be on hand for emergencies during the event.

One Week before the Event

❏ Send an updated press release with a photograph or illustration to the media. Include any new noteworthy information, such as celebrities or dignitaries expected to attend.

❏ Make follow-up calls to media five days before the event. Keep calling until you have definite commitments from the media for coverage.

❑ Confirm refreshments, audio equipment, seating, rest-rooms, first aid, photographer, supplies, flowers, decor, entertainment, etc.

❑ Update RSVP list daily.

❑ Keep in daily contact with the caterer as the number of RSVPs will change hourly.

❑ Write a step-by-step agenda for the big day.

❑ Conduct a dress rehearsal of the event from start to finish.

❑ Double-check action items on your assignment lists.

❑ If possible, have the keynote speaker rehearse. If this is not feasible, make sure that he or she knows what to do from the moment of arrival through departure.

❑ Know how long everyone will be speaking so you can plan a realistic agenda.

Day of the Event

❑ Be organized so that you can start on time.

❑ Distribute agenda to keynote speakers. Make sure they know what to do.

❑ Set up media registration table.

❑ Have a stack of media kits on hand for the press.

❑ Have guests sign in, if appropriate.

❑ Provide greeters or ushers.

❑ Follow your agenda.

❑ Circulate, meet as many people as possible.

❑ Pass out information.

❑ Allow for extra time in case something goes wrong.

❑ Provide transportation for any dignitaries and guest speakers who need it.

❑ Make copies of your guest list for future uses.

If You Have to Put on Your Event FAST!

⟨≡ **Tip**

The key to success is a motivated, organized committee.

Sometimes—eek!—you will have much less time than you'd like to pull together an event. Round up a crew of dynamic people whom you can trust to follow through on their commitments and bring them together for a meeting within two days of deciding you'll put on an event.

Four Weeks before an Event

☐ Select and invite committee members to a meeting.

☐ Delegate authority on written assignment sheets for each committee and know where and what everyone is doing for the event and at the event.

☐ Determine timeline needed to accomplish each event.

☐ Draw up a "Responsibility/Status Report" (see chart).

☐ Make sure you have everyone's home and office phone and fax numbers, as well as their e-mail addresses.

☐ Select date, time, and location.

☐ Decide on budget. Many charity fund-raisers don't have a budget per se because they count on donations to supply everything they need for the event. A party with several hosts may need close scrutiny by your treasurer and finance committee. Costs should be identified and confirmed.

☐ Determine if you want to set up a Web site for the event.

☐ Select and invite keynote speaker(s) or entertainment.

☐ Arrange for menu, photographer, audio equipment, seating, restrooms, first aid, supplies, decor, entertainment.

❑ Make sure you have parking to accommodate expected guests. For a more formal event, or where space is limited, you may want to offer valet parking.

❑ Check to see if you need insurance and county or state licenses (e.g., for selling or serving liquor).

❑ Select and order souvenirs.

❑ Have a backup for outdoor events in case of inclement weather.

❑ Compile a guest list of friends, media, local dignitaries, and celebrities as well as area businesspeople and potential customers.

❑ Meet with chairs of charities, civic groups, and political organizations for their advice concerning what has worked well and what hasn't in the community.

❑ Compile a notebook with all your information (i.e., to-do lists, phone numbers of suppliers, correspondence) for easy reference.

❑ Post signs in public places announcing the event (if open to the public).

❑ Reserve mobile phones or walkie-talkies for staff to keep in touch with each other during the event if logistics warrant it.

❑ Schedule a medical professional, such as a company nurse, to be on hand for emergencies during the event.

❑ Order invitations.

Tip

Always hold outside events under a tent. You never can tell about the weather.

Three Weeks before the Event

❏ Write a newsworthy press release.

❏ Prepare and send out to media an impressive press kit that includes the press release, history of the organization, photographs, and brochures.

❏ Follow up on publicity.

❏ Review assignments with staff for day of the event.

❏ Mail invitations, with phone numbers to RSVP and explicit directions, to all guests.

One Week before the Event

❏ Send an updated press release to media. Include any new noteworthy information, such as celebrities expected to attend.

❏ Make follow-up calls to media five days before the event. Keep calling until you have definite commitments for media coverage.

❏ Confirm refreshments, audio equipment, seating, restrooms, first aid, photographer, supplies, flowers, decor, entertainment, etc.

❏ Have a trial tasting of the food planned for the menu.

❏ Reserve walkie-talkies for committee to keep in touch with each other during the event if logistics warrant it.

❏ Update RSVP list daily.

❏ Keep in daily contact with the caterer as the number of RSVPs will change hourly.

❏ Write a step-by-step agenda—a staging guide—for the big day (p. 58).

❏ Plan how to conclude the event, and end the event at a specific time.

❑ Conduct a dress rehearsal/sound check of the event from start to finish.

❑ Double-check action items on your assignment sheets.

❑ If possible, have the keynote speaker rehearse. If this is not feasible, make sure that he or she knows what to do from the moment of arrival through departure.

Day of the Event

❑ Be organized and prompt.

❑ Set up media registration table with press kits.

❑ Have guests sign in.

❑ Provide greeters or ushers.

❑ Follow your agenda.

❑ Distribute agenda to keynote speakers, participants, and core committee.

❑ Know how long everyone will be speaking.

❑ Circulate, meet as many people as possible.

❑ Distribute appropriate information.

❑ Provide transportation if necessary for dignitaries, guest speakers.

❑ Make copies of the guest list for future uses.

A Gala Event!

Sample Responsibility/Status Report

Event: _____

Current Date: _____

Report Date: _____
(the date when committee members will have
to meet and report on the status of their work)

Item	Responsibility	Due Date	Status
Order invitations	Anderson		Done
Compile mailing list	Gordon		Done
Calligraphy for envelopes	Anderson		Arranged
Mail out invitations	Anderson	12/2	
Track RSVPs	Widem		OK
Arrange for music	Cohen		Done
Order flowers	Cohen		Done
Order food & beverages	Asen		Done
Coordinate parking	Stanley		OK
Secure photographer	Asen		Reviewing portfolios
Set up facility tour	Stanley	11/28	
Recruit greeters	Widem	12/15	
Agenda/program	Hughes	12/1	
Order souvenirs	Ivanoff		Done
Write press release	Lee	11/28	
Mail press kits	Miller	12/1	
Pre-event follow-up w/press	Lee	12/10	

Sample Staging Guideline

Time	What Happens
4:15 PM	Decorations picked up from suppliers
5:00	Balloons delivered
	Garage opens
	Kitchen items delivered
	Live auction props delivered
	Setup begins
5:15	Beverage delivered
	Food delivered
	Auction items delivered
5:30	Registration table set
6:00	Kitchen set
6:30	Bar set
	Decorations complete and final
	Coffee set
	Registration set
	Food table set
	Silent auction set
6:45	Hot food goes on buffet table
7:00	Music and dancing opens
	Registration opens
	Silent auction opens
8:00	Auctioneer arrives
8:10	5-minute warning for closing of Table 1 (Getaways)
8:15	Check-out set
	Table 1 closes; bid sheets to check-out
	5-minute warning for closing of Table 2 (Services)

(continued next page)

Sample Staging Guideline (continued)

Time	What Happens
8:20 PM	Table 2 closes; bid sheets to check-out
8:30	Check-out for winning bids opens
8:30	Registration closes
8:50	Last call for beverages
8:55	Last call for raffle tickets
9:00	End of beverage service Raffle closes
9:15	Raffle winner envelope w/cash to podium
9:25	John V. to ask guests to pull chairs to stage area for live auction
9:30	Sale table (of discounted items that didn't receive any bids on Tables 1 or 2) closes—bid sheets to check-out Sara M. takes microphone to say thank-yous
9:35	Raffle winner chosen before opening of live auction
9:38	Live auction begins
10:00	Live auction closes Check-out continues Clean-up begins
11:59	Garage closes

Under the Honorary Patronage of

First Lady Hillary Rodham Clinton

the Committee

requests the pleasure of your company

at

The Thirty-first Annual

Meridian Ball

Friday, the fifteenth of October

nine-thirty o'clock

Meridian House

1630 Crescent Place, Northwest

Washington, District of Columbia

Preceded by Embassy dinners

Black Tie

Thirty-first Annual
Meridian Ball

The Honorable
Mary Mel French
Honorary Chairman

Hagel   Mrs. Patrick J. Leahy
Co-Chairmen

Advisory Committee

er	Hon. Penne Percy Korth
	Mrs. Joseph I. Lieberman
n	Mrs. Sam A. Nunn
h	Mrs. Jean Kurth Oberstar
	Mrs. Michael G. Oxley
	Mrs. Jefferson Patterson
	Mrs. Barbara F. Richardson
	Mrs. Richard W. Riley
	Mrs. Tim Roemer
er	Mrs. Joseph H. Santarlasci Jr.
	Mrs. Ronald E. Sappenfield
	Mrs. Bob L. Schieffer
	Mrs. Rodney E. Slater
	Hon. Jane DeGraff Sloat
	Mrs. Ted Stevens
	Mrs. John S. Tanner
	Mrs. Richard L. Thompson
	Mrs. Charles Swan Weber
omo	Mrs. Togo D. West Jr.
	Mrs. James McSherry Wimsatt

on. Thomas J. Tauke
Business Committee

## Chapter 5

Building Your Contacts

One of your most important tools for staging a successful event is contacts—who you and members of your event team know (or come to know) among leaders in the community and media. The ability to make contacts and use them well is a vital key to your event's success!

You will need to develop two important contact lists:

- Fund-raising list
- Media list

Charity Membership

On the fund-raising list, include people who might be interested in your project. Coming up with this list is easier than you think. Put on your thinking cap, brainstorm with your event team, and make a list of names, addresses, and phone numbers of people who come to mind when you think about the charity. Begin the list with clients, friends, and neighbors who are active, outgoing, and community-service oriented. Also, make a list of city officials, local business owners, and interest groups. For a fund-raising campaign, the list could look like this:

- Rotary Clubs
- Chamber of Commerce
- Museum guilds
- Hospital guilds
- Women's clubs
- Lions Clubs
- Philanthropic organizations
- Professional organizations

Some of these organizations may already support the cause that you have selected. Great! You can contact the local chapter and ask for help with your event. Discuss your overlapping interests and coordinate efforts.

 **Tip**

Obtaining access to a variety of organizations' mailing lists is a powerful reason to include people on your event team who are already active in the community.

Ask all members on the event team to contribute the membership rosters of any groups they belong to. It's far easier for a member of the country club to ask for permission to use the list for a charity than for a stranger to come in and request use of the list.

If you are the chairman of a national event, get people from different states to refer you to individuals experienced in fund-raising. It is essential to bring in people who know each region. For example, if your corporation has decided to put on a national function, call groups on your contact list in each state. Explain that you are looking for a community leader to serve on a national committee. If the executive director of the group you are calling does not have the time to serve, ask that person to recommend someone else who could.

This research takes time, and the larger the project, the longer it takes. It is time consuming, but it pays off. A list of people you and your event team know is a terrific starting point for building the mailing list for the event. Find out if the charity has a national or state office. Obtain their local mailing list to add to your database.

Remember to tell people—everyone!—about the event. They will get excited too. Let others help build the mailing list: Everyone knows someone who may be interested in participating.

Organize the list by categories, including city officials, business leaders, clients, neighbors, friends, and organizations. You will refer to it many, many times.

Media List

Compile a list of media contacts at newspapers, magazines, radio stations, and TV stations—both local and national if your event is a larger effort. Construct a calendar of when you will send press releases and other material to each media contact.

- Begin with your contacts and add to the list.
- Go to the library and ask the reference librarian for help in finding listings of local media. (See suggestions below.)

Your media contacts are important for two reasons:

1. They increase community awareness of the beneficiary institution's charity efforts and how the event will help them.

2. They increase community awareness of your company or organization, which can bolster overall support or business throughout the year.

Your Media Contact List

For each media outlet in your area, collect the following information:

Newspaper

Name of newspaper _____

Telephone number _____

Address _____

Fax number _____

E-mail address _____

Name and phone number of
lifestyle editor _____

Name and phone number of
business editor _____

Name and phone number of
community news/community
calendar editor _____

Name and phone number of
photo editor _____

Magazine

Name of magazine _____

Telephone number _____

Address _____

Fax number _____

E-mail address _____

Name and phone number of
lifestyle editor _____

Name and phone number of
business editor _____

Name and phone number of
community news/community
calendar editor _____

Name and phone number of
photo editor _____

(continued next page)

Your Media Contact List (*continued*)

Radio

Station call letters _____

Telephone number _____

Address _____

Fax _____

News assignment editor _____

Phone number _____

E-mail _____

Producer _____

Phone number _____

E-mail _____

Television

Station call letters _____

Telephone number _____

Address _____

Fax _____

News assignment editor _____

Phone number _____

E-mail _____

Producer _____

Phone number _____

E-mail _____

- The reference section of your public library can help you get started with this list. The reference librarian can help you find directories of the media in your area. A common one is Bacon's Media Directory; other references are the Gale Directory of Publications and

Broadcast Media, Gebbie Press All-in-One Directory, and Working Press of the Nation.

- Another source of media information is the city government. Often a community service division has compiled this information for public use.

- Don't forget the free "throwaway" newspapers. It's very important to use every resource available. These papers reach many households. Make sure cable stations are on your list, too. Find out which public access station serves your area.

 **Tip**

When you get your event team together, team members should brainstorm about the local media outlets, mostly to cull any that shouldn't be on the list.

- In a metropolitan area with many media outlets, you might want to concentrate your efforts on specific newspapers, magazines, and radio and TV stations that serve the audience you expect to attract to the event.

- Once you compile the list, call each newspaper, magazine, and TV and radio station to confirm that the information is correct. Personnel change frequently in the news business. You want to make sure your well-crafted press releases are going to the right person!

- When you are calling to double-check names, titles, and phone numbers, ask how each media outlet prefers to receive material. Fax? E-mail?

- Ask each newspaper and magazine what kind of photographs it prefers (black-and-white or color, glossy or matte, digital).

- If you don't understand how a news organization assigns and covers stories, ask. Generally at a radio station, the news director gets the news people together and hands out assignments. The program director organizes the material for the show. At a newspaper, different editors handle different sections in the paper. For example, there are business, metro, and style editors. The nature of the event dictates which editors receive the press releases. If you are sponsoring a class on baking bread and donating the proceeds to a cause, you'll send information to the business and food editors. Always send information to the editors handling community news and the community calendar.

- Record this information in the media contact list. Don't rely on your memory when dealing with so many entities for weeks and months.

400 Kousa Dogwood Trees
Lining the Leesburg By-Pass

When you participate
in this event, you help create
a more beautiful community
for all of us to enjoy.

Please consider this a legacy
you can leave in your name,
or in memory of a loved one.

Each purchase of a tree will include
a ticket to an event to celebrate

The First Planting of the Trees:

The Harlequin Dogwood Ball

The Dogwood Committee has selected the
Kousa Dogwood, recommended by the State
Forestry Service because of its ability to withstand
traffic volume and other elements native to this area.
The trees will be approximately one-half by 6 feet
and planted 40 feet apart.

The funding for this beautification program
will come from corporate and private contributions
which are tax-deductible.

A commemorative plaque inscribed with the contributors'
names will be installed at the Town Hall of Leesburg.

Each purchase of a tree for $125.00 includes a ticket
to the Harlequin Ball to be held on October 16, 1999.

October 16, 1999

at the Leesburg Airport
Beechcraft Hanger

Reception 7:00 pm
Followed by Dinner, Dancing
and Entertainment

Black Tie (optional)

For more information, please call:
703-737-7002

Invitation to Follow

## Chapter 6

Media Relations

A press release is a very powerful tool. But it is not enough. In addition to the written word, you must make personal contacts within each media outlet. The media committee on your event team can be very helpful here. Recruit people who have media experience because they can get to the right people when they approach newspapers, magazines, and radio and TV stations about the event. But do not despair if you have a crew of beginners. The rules of the road are the same—it may just take longer for newcomers to navigate it!

If you are on the media team, whether you have contacts already or not, you need to call the local media and set up appointments. Bring with you all the material that might be useful in explaining the event or charity to the news person:

 **Tip**

People's names are extremely important to them. Make sure you get spellings and titles correct.

- Press release
- Fact sheet about your company or auxiliary
- Charity brochure (if one is available from the charity you are supporting)
- Picture of a company representative with the charity spokesperson
- Picture of someone being helped by the cause you are supporting

In dealing with the print or broadcast media person:

- Tell the media representative why his or her audience should be interested in a story featuring your company or organization. Highlight facts about both the organization and the cause for which you are raising money, goods, or services.

- Follow up the appointment with a note thanking the media representative for his or her time. A few days later, call to ask if there is anything you can supply him or her. Once you have established a rapport with the local media, you should keep them tied into your pipeline of activities, projects, and charity work.

- Always be honest and sincere when you are dealing with the media. Never lie. If you don't know the answer to a question, tell the media representative you will find out the answer.

- Point out possible feature stories about the organization and the charity you are supporting. The more creative you are in presenting something newsworthy about your event, the more likely the media will pick up on it. People are busy; give them a lead and they'll take it.

- Find out who is in charge of the community calendar and make sure your event is included.

Press Releases

Every press release and press campaign should follow these guidelines:

- The press release must be typed, double-spaced, on 8½" x 11" letterhead.
- It must be timely. Announce the event early and then send a release right before it takes place.
- Immediately after the event, send a press release to describe the actual event.
- Invite the press to attend a variety of events, whether it is your big function or a series of events that lead up to a longer fund-raising campaign.

 **Tip**

Photographs say a thousand words—make sure your image sends a lively, interesting message!

- Whenever possible, send a photograph.
- Show action in the photograph. A CEO wielding a hammer on a home for Habitat for Humanity is going to make the photo editor happier than a shot of two men in suits shaking hands. And as the New York advertising agencies know, a sure-fire winner includes animals or children in the picture.
- Ask the cause you're supporting if any photographs are available.
- Although you can hire photographers, look for an experienced photobug who is a member of your committee or broader organization.

 **Tip**

Make the life of the newspaper and magazine editors as easy as possible. The more convenient it is to use your material, the more likely the editors will select it.

- Ask each newspaper and magazine on the media list what type of photograph they prefer. In the past, newspapers needed black-and-white glossy-finished prints. Improved technology and increased use of color in newspapers mean that they can use color slides and prints, as do magazines. Publications are also moving to digitized images, so if you have a scanner or a digital camera, find out if the publication can handle electronic transfer of photographs.
- Send photos or videos to the television stations with press releases. Visuals are crucial in television, and TV can be a powerful source in promoting the event.
- Review the model press releases that follow to see how many different versions of a press release may be written.

Public Service Announcements (PSAs)

The Federal Communications Commission requires TV and radio stations to give a certain amount of free air time as a public service. Capitalize on this free advertisement opportunity by sending your local stations public service announcements (PSAs) they will want to air.

- Write two PSAs to send to local radio and TV stations based on the examples that follow on pp. 86–87. Ten- and 30-second PSAs are the most common length for these messages, which serve as free commercials.

- To get the most impact out of PSAs, they need to be read every day for two weeks before your event.

- Mail two copies of each PSA to radio and TV stations, and follow up with a phone call.

- If you have a good relation with the radio and television stations, try to arrange for a live "interview" for you to "chat" on the air about your event. In some media markets, perhaps you can drop by the station each day to talk about an upcoming charity event.

 **Tip**

Many organizations are now doing two-minute video news releases. Send a video news release along with out-takes—the footage that wasn't used in the video itself—which is known as the B roll.

- With technology being more accessible to everyone, radio and TV stations are becoming more amenable to using videos and audiotapes. Talk to the stations and find out how they feel about video news releases. Sometimes the station will even be willing to produce a tape for you.

News Press Advisory

A press advisory is a one-page "quickie" sent to print and electronic media to alert them to an event. It is the bare bones of a press release, limited to Who, What, When, Where and Why.

- When you call to confirm that the media mailing list is up to date, find out if they accept news advisories and what form each publication or station would like them in.

- Mail or fax it; more and more editors like to be e-mailed.

Following Up

- Call after sending a press release to make sure the news outlet got the release.
- Call the day before the event to remind them of the particulars and to find out if someone from the station or paper will be covering it. Ask if the reporter will be bringing a camera crew or photographer, or whether you should send pictures.
- Call the day of the event.
- Call after the event to see if they need any more information.
- And if you tell someone you are going to get back to him or her with information or material, do it. People in the media understand that it is your business to promote the event. It is also your job to be professional, courteous, and reliable.

 **Tip**

Make your media list and follow up, follow up, follow up each and every time you make a media contact. This is absolutely vital.

Skeleton of a Press Release

A press release has a standard format.

- Use 8½" x 11" letterhead.
- Use margins that are at least 1 inch all the way around.
- At the top left of the page, put the contact information (name, title, phone number), single-spaced.
- Writing "For immediate release" at the top of the page on the right margin lets the editor know the information

can be used immediately. Skip two lines and write a headline.

- Center the headline and put it in bold type.
- In the headline, use active verbs and information-packed nouns to convey the news aspect of the event and to catch an editor's interest immediately.
- Two lines down from the headline, begin the copy with a dateline: date, city, and state.
- Double-space the text of the press release.
- Try to confine the press release to one page, double-spaced.
- Include a quotation from someone in your organization.
- End the release with three hatch marks (# # #) or the notation -30-. This tells the editor the copy is complete.
- If the release runs to two pages, at the bottom of the first page, write —more—. On the second page, in the top left corner, place a "slug"—one or two words that identify the story and put ADD 1 or PAGE 2 on the next line down. Skip two lines and finish the release.
- Double-check to make sure you have spelled everyone's name and title correctly. This is crucial!

On the next page after the sample skeleton of a press release are models that have been fleshed out with information. The names and companies are fictitious, but they will give you a format to follow in writing your own.

A Gala Event!

Sample Skeleton of a Press Release

NAME OF CONTACT, TITLE
NAME OF COMPANY (IF NOT ON LETTERHEAD)
TELEPHONE NUMBER   FOR IMMEDIATE RELEASE

HEADLINE FOR THE PRESS RELEASE

Date, City, State — Who, what, when, where, and why should be covered in the first paragraph—or, occasionally, the first two paragraphs. Present this information in short, easy-to read sentences.

The second paragraph can be a continuation of the information in the first sentence or an elaboration. This is a good place to detail the reason the event is taking place.

A quotation from someone in your organization can go next. Make sure you spell the person's name correctly and include the person's title.

Include a paragraph about the charity or cause you are supporting.

Always end the text by giving the name and phone number of the person the media can contact for more information.

# # #

The names and company information in this press release are fictitious. Use it as a model for announcing a product your organization has designed for the event.

Sample Press Release 1: Special Product

JUANITA BLAKE, VICE PRESIDENT
CORPORATE COMMUNICATIONS
(555) 555-5555   FOR IMMEDIATE RELEASE

EXCLUSIVE HAT DESIGNED TO BENEFIT PARKS

March 25, San Jose, Calif.—Hats on Every Head, Inc., unveiled its new hat, "Fancy's Choice," at the company's annual convention held earlier this year in Las Vegas.

"Fancy's Choice," which features silk California poppies as its crowning glory, is a playful creation in tribute to garden parties everywhere. Hats on Every Head, Inc., will donate a portion of the proceeds to the state's Park Beautification Program.

"California poppies are known for their charm and exuberant color," says Heather Hatmaiden, president and CEO of the company. "The energy this flower brings to the landscape should inspire all to keep beautifying the environment around us," says Hatmaiden.

Initiated in 1939, the California Park Beautification Program works to keep the median strips as well as neighborhood parks clean and attractive. For more information, contact Juanita Blake at (555) 555-5555.

# # #

This press release, using fictitious names and information, is a model for announcing a public speaking engagement.

Sample Press Release 2: Speaking Engagement

OTIS BAKER
DIRECTOR OF COMMUNICATIONS
(555) 555-5555   FOR IMMEDIATE RELEASE

HOSPITAL GUILD TO BENEFIT THE REED MEMORIAL

April 1, San Jose, Calif.—The Reed Memorial Hospital Guild is seeking the support from the community to help Reed Memorial Hospital staff provide a room in the Emergency Care area for children. To their appeal for broad-based support, representatives from the hospital guild will speak on October 3rd at 2:00 P.M. to the San Jose Garden Club and ask for support in putting on a fund-raiser.

"The Children's Emergency Care Room, with its pleasant colors, toys and smaller equipment both soothes a sick child and ensures that the care Reed Memorial Hospital provides is the best possible for our smallest patients," says Edna Goodmedicine, director of the Reed Memorial Hospital Guild. "Though beneficial, the program is expensive. We want to do our part to help, and we hope the San Jose Garden Club will join our efforts," she adds.

The Reed Memorial Hospital Guild is conducting a regional campaign to promote Children's Emergency Care Room, Goodmedicine said.

To attend this speaking engagement or to help the Reed Memorial Hospital Guild, contact Otis Baker, director of communications, at (555) 555-5555.

# # #

Sample Press Release 3: Formal Dinner

MARIE BITZOW, VICE PRESIDENT
CORPORATE COMMUNICATIONS
(555) 555-5555   FOR IMMEDIATE RELEASE

BLACK TIE DINNER WILL BENEFIT LEADER DOGS FOR THE BLIND

March 7, Hallajah, Ohio—Simple Simon Pie Company will host a black tie dinner at 8 p.m. June 1 at the Holly Hills Wood Hotel to benefit the charity organization Leader Dogs for the Blind.

Leader Dogs for the Blind is a nonprofit organization developed to minimize the disability of blindness. Founded in 1939, the organization trains dogs to lead blind people through everyday situations that are often hazardous. The blind are consequently given more travel freedom and independence. The cost to Leader Dogs for the Blind for this service is approximately $11,000 per dog.

To help, Simple Simon Pie will host a black tie dinner. The company is charging the public $100.00 per person, with proceeds going to Leader Dogs for the Blind.

Other groups and organizations planning to attend the fund-raiser will be Kiwanis, the Long Branch PTA Board, the Sprinklerdale Civic Association and the Presleyville Old Hound Dog Club.

For more information, contact Marie Bitzow at (555) 555-5555.

# # #

NOTE: If you plan to hold some activity other than a dinner, change the word "dinner" to describe your function. This press release, like all others, is only for suggestions.

Sample Press Release 4: Seminar/Workshop

GEORGE ALBERT
LONG BRANCH PTA
(555) 555-5555   FOR IMMEDIATE RELEASE

SCRAPBOOK SEMINAR WILL UPGRADE
ELEMENTARY SCHOOL LIBRARY

Feb. 13, Dublin, Ind.—The Long Branch Elementary School PTA will host a Creative Scrapbook workshop to raise money for the school's media center. The workshop will take place on March 14 in the school cafeteria, 1434 Ivy League St., Dublin.

The PTA has been focusing their yearlong campaign on helping upgrade the school library, which needs microfiche machines, computers, film strips, overhead projectors, and new compact disks.

To help, a Creative Scrapbook workshop will be given by the PTA. Members of the public are being charged $12.00 per person, which covers the cost of instruction and supplies. The proceeds will go to the school library fund.

Workshop participants will learn how to create a scrapbook that highlights each individual's personality. They will also learn the proper way to preserve photographs, newspaper clippings, and other memorabilia.

Other groups and organizations planning to attend this fund-raising workshop will be the Cambridge Public Librarian Association and the Lions Club.

Any individuals who would like to attend the workshop or contribute to this worthy charity should call George Albert at (555) 555-5555.

# # #

NOTE: If you plan to hold an event other than a workshop, change the wording to reflect your function. This press release, like all the others, is only for suggestions. Feel free to write your own press releases so that your group gets the most recognition possible. Where it says "Other groups and organizations planning to attend this fund-raising workshop," you should list organizations, groups, etc., planning on attending or contributing.

Sample Press Release 5: Before a Speaking Engagement

HARRY BLAKE, VICE PRESIDENT
PET VETS, INC.
(555) 555-5555   FOR IMMEDIATE RELEASE

PET VETS, INC., SEEKS SUPPORT OF FRATERNITY
TO BENEFIT CHARITY

June 3, Dayton, Ohio—Pet Vets, Inc., is seeking the support from the community to help Leader Dogs for the Blind, a not-for-profit charity that breeds and trains guide dogs for the blind. To make an impact, veterinarians from the Pet Vets clinic will speak on August 3 at 7:30 P.M. to the Alpha Omega fraternity board to ask for their support in putting on a fund-raiser.

"The Leader Dog program successfully provides hundreds of guide dogs to blind people every year, making life for the blind a little easier," says Molly Baker of Pet Vets, Inc. "Though beneficial, the program is very expensive. We want to do our part to help and hope the Alpha Omega fraternity will join our efforts."

Pet Vets, Inc., is putting on a national campaign to promote Leader Dogs for the Blind. Molly Baker, vice president for the company, said, "Pet Vets selected this charity to help, not only because we think it is so deserving, but because the money is so well spent. Only 3 percent of funding is deducted to cover administrative costs."

To attend this speech or to help Leader Dogs for the Blind, contact Harry Blake at (555) 555-5555.

# # #

Note: The names of people and individuals in this sample press release are fictitious. Customize the release to meet your needs.

Sample Press Release 6: After a Speaking Engagement

HARRY BLAKE, VICE PRESIDENT
PET VETS, INC.
(555) 555-5555   FOR IMMEDIATE RELEASE

ALPHA OMEGA FRATERNITY JOINS PET VETS, INC., IN SUPPORTING LEADER DOGS FOR THE BLIND

August 4, Dayton, Ohio—Molly Baker of Pet Vets, Inc., spoke to the Alpha Omega fraternity executive board on August 3 in an effort to join forces and hold a fund-raiser for the charity organization Leader Dogs for the Blind.

As a result of the meeting, Alpha Omega will staff the bar at the Pet Vets' Capital Cat Competition being held August 16 at the state fairground.

Jeff Baron, president of the club, said, "We are very proud to be part of something so worthwhile and that will benefit the blind."

Founded in 1939, Leader Dogs for the Blind is headquartered in Rochester, Michigan. The program/organization assists the handicapped by providing guide dogs to the blind. The services offered by this program include breeding, training, and a replacement dog, if necessary. The cost for this service is $11,000 per dog.

The dogs protect against everyday travel hazards and minimize the disability of blindness, permitting an individual to go where he wants to go, when he wants to go, thus increasing independence and job opportunities for the blind person.

Individuals or organizations interested in helping Leader Dogs for the Blind should contact Harry Blake at (555) 555-5555.

-30-

Sample Press Release 7: After the Event

JUANITA BLAKE, VICE PRESIDENT
CORPORATE COMMUNICATIONS
(555) 555-5555   FOR IMMEDIATE RELEASE

PARK BEAUTIFICATION FUND-RAISER A COMPLETE SUCCESS

September 12, San Diego, Calif.—Local Hats on Every Head franchise owners hosted a black tie dinner-dance on September 11 to benefit the California Park Beautification Program. The dinner raised $50,000 for the charity.

Four hundred people attended the gala dinner in the Carlton-Hayword Plaza Suites, which featured famous singer Mr. Beau Flowers as a keynote speaker. Mr. Flowers has been a long-time advocate of the Parks Beautification Program.

Initiated in 1939, the Park Beautification Program works to keep the median strips as well as neighborhood parks clean and attractive.

"We felt the dinner was a huge success," said Heather Hatmaiden, president and CEO of the company. "Everyone enjoyed listening to Mr. Flowers and the other entertainers who performed during the evening. We are very pleased to be presenting the proceeds of the dinner to a worthy cause."

Some of the local groups that helped make the dinner so successful were the Bridgemont Bridge Club, the Hollyhocks Hills PTA, and the 49s Golden Girl Society.

Hats on Every Head has been working on a statewide campaign to benefit the California Parks Beautification Program. The company's vice president and director of design, Sally Sosmart, designed "Fancy's Choice," a hat that pays tribute to the sunny disposition of the California poppy. The hat was displayed during the dinner, and Hats on Every Head will continue to donate a portion of the proceeds from hat sales to the state Park Beautification Program.

For more information on the hat or the dinner, contact Juanita Blake, vice president of corporate communications at Hats on Every Head, (555) 555-5555.

-30-

Public Service Announcements

You send public service announcements (PSAs) to radio stations. Ten-seconds and 30-seconds are standard lengths for these brief messages that the radio announcer will read over the air. When you are calling to double-check names and phone numbers of radio stations, you should also ask if the station has a preference for the length of PSAs.

PSAs have a specific format. By following this format, you show the radio station that you have done your homework and respect its standard presentation. Anything that makes the life of an announcer easier is appreciated—and rewarded with on-air announcements! FCC regulations require radio stations to devote a percentage of their air time to public service content. The radio stations need you as much as you need them!

Two sample PSAs on pp. 86–87 illustrate the correct format. Also included are alternative messages, showing how the same information can be relayed a little differently. Personalize these PSAs to reflect your own information (company, event, etc.). If you are involved in a long-term campaign, you will need to send fresh PSAs to the radio stations from time to time. There are some general guidelines to the PSAs you send out:

- Send the PSAs out on letterhead.
- Triple space (except between ANNCR: and the body of the message).
- Use very wide margins.
- Always write in capital letters.
- Send each TV/radio station several extra copies of the script.
- If you send out an audio or video cassette, include several copies of the script with the tape.

Here are the different parts of the PSAs.

- Your name and phone number are typed in the top right corner in case the station has any questions.

- The next number below that on the left margin is the time it takes to read the commercial. For a 10-second spot, it will read :10. For a 30-second spot, it will read :30.

- The "Kill Date" is the last date the PSA should be read on the air. In this case, it should be the date the event is to take place.

- "ANNCR" is the announcer, or disc jockey, who will read the PSA over the air.

- The message you send should be personalized for your event.

- 0-0-0, 0-0-0-0 is where you should substitute your phone number. Include the hyphens between each digit.

- The last number—in parentheses ( )—is the number of words in the text.

A Gala Event!

Sample Public Service Announcements

Your Name
Phone Number

:10

KILL DATE: **DATE OF EVENT**

ANNCR:

HELP **NAME OF YOUR COMPANY** SUPPORT **NAME OF**

CHARITY OR EVENT.

COME TO **EVENT** ON **DATE AND TIME**.

CALL **0-0-0, 0-0-0-0** FOR DETAILS   (24)

Your Name
Phone Number

:30

KILL DATE: **DATE OF EVENT**

ANNCR:

HELP UNITE THE BLIND WITH LEADER DOGS. **THE**

COMPANY NAME WILL SPONSOR A BLACK TIE DINNER

TO BENEFIT **LEADER DOGS FOR THE BLIND**, A NONPROFIT

ORGANIZATION THAT PROVIDES GUIDE DOGS TO THE

BLIND. THE DINNER WILL BE **DATE AND TIME**. GET

INVOLVED BY CALLING **0-0-0, 0-0-0-0** FOR DETAILS.

(47)

10-Second Spots for You to Choose From and Insert in Sample PSA:

HELP (THE COMPANY NAME) SUPPORT (CHARITY). COME TO A (NAME OF OR TYPE OF EVENT) ON (DATE) AND (TIME). CALL 0-0-0, 0-0-0-0 FOR DETAILS.   (25)

THE PATTYPAT HAT COMPANY URGES YOU TO SUPPORT LEADER DOGS FOR THE BLIND BY ATTENDING A DINNER ON FEBRUARY 24 AT 8 P.M. CALL 0-0-0, 0-0-0-0 FOR DETAILS.   (24)

COME TO A BLACK TIE DINNER HOSTED BY PATTYPAT HAT COMPANY TO BENEFIT LEADER DOGS FOR THE BLIND. GET INVOLVED BY CALLING 0-0-0, 0-0-0-0.   (23)

30-Second Spots for You to Choose From and Format Like Sample PSA:

HELP UNITE THE BLIND WITH LEADER DOGS. PATTYPAT HAT COMPANY WILL SPONSOR A BLACK TIE DINNER TO BENEFIT LEADER DOGS FOR THE BLIND, A NONPROFIT ORGANIZATION THAT PROVIDES GUIDE DOGS TO THE BLIND. THE DINNER WILL BE FEBRUARY 24 AT 8 P.M. GET INVOLVED BY CALLING 0-0-0, 0-0-0-0 FOR DETAILS.   (47)

PATTYPAT HAT COMPANY WILL HOST A BLACK TIE DINNER TO BENEFIT LEADER DOGS FOR THE BLIND. THIS NONPROFIT ORGANIZATION PROVIDES BLIND PEOPLE WITH LEADER DOGS SO THAT THE BLIND CAN FUNCTION MORE INDEPENDENTLY IN SOCIETY. FOR MORE INFORMATION, CALL 0-0-0, 0-0-0-0.   (40)

A BLACK TIE DINNER WILL BE HELD TO BENEFIT THE LEADER DOGS FOR THE BLIND ORGANIZATION. PATTYPAT HAT COMPANY WILL HOST THE EVENT ON FEBRUARY 24 AT 8 P.M. INDIVIDUALS AND ORGANIZATIONS CAN HELP BY CALLING 0-0-0, 0-0-0-0. MINIMIZE THE HANDICAP OF BLINDNESS AND GET INVOLVED.   (45)

Sample News Media Advisory

NEWS MEDIA ADVISORY

News Media Contact: (Name and number)

Headline: (Who is doing what? [e.g., FASHION SEMINAR TO BENEFIT HABITAT FOR HUMANITY])

WHO (Name of group sponsoring event [e.g., Hats on Every Head])

(Information on your local business, i.e., # years in operation, area of service, any publicity received, etc.)

WHAT (Event being sponsored [e.g., FASHION SEMINAR TO BENEFIT HABITAT FOR HUMANITY])

(Title of workshop [e.g., '98 Topping It Off]) seminar offered to the general public. Attendees will learn about (blurb on content of workshop—slide presentation, vignettes or samples available, etc.). Donations collected at the door will benefit (name of charity) (e.g., Habitat for Humanity [HFHI]). All donations are tax deductible.

WHEN (Date, Time)

WHERE (Location, Room Name, etc.)

CONTACT (Contact Name, and Phone Number)

Information about the charity: Founded in 1976, HFHI is dedicated to eliminating poverty housing worldwide. In an effort to stand up to its social responsibility, Hats on Every Head has established a partnership with HFHI to assist in fulfilling the mission of "Building Houses and Building Lives."

Donations may also be mailed directly to HFHI at P.O. Box 841, SC 02131, Americus, GA 31709. All donations are tax deductible.

Sample of Fact Sheet on Company

This is a fictitious company. Customize the fact sheet to suit your organization.

Facts About Hats on Every Head

Established: 1982

CEO and President: Heather Hatmaiden

Product: Hats and accessories.

Number of Outlets: 45 shops operate throughout California.

New Product for Charity: "Fancy's Choice"—designed and created to support the California Park Beautification Program.

Company History: Heather Hatmaiden established Hats on Every Head as a project while earning her MBA from San Diego State University. She began with designs for three original hats, and sales were brisk enough to convince her that a shop was viable. The Hats on Every Head designer line has expanded to more than 20. Hats on Every Head also sells hats from a variety of manufacturers, offering customers a wide range from which to choose.

Lewis Allen

Lewis Allen produces for the theatre, motion pictures and television. A native of Virginia, he attended the University of Virginia (Phi Beta Kappa), and is the recipient of an honorary doctorate degree from Shenandoah University. During World War II, Lewis Allen served in the United States Air Force in the Middle East, North Africa and Europe.

Among Lewis Allen's numerous theatre productions are Broadway hit, Master Class; Vita and Virginia; Tru; A Few Good Men; I am not Rapport; Sam Shepard's A Lie of The Mind; The Big Love; the Quintero/Robards revival of The Iceman Cometh; Annie, coproduced with Mike Nichols; My one and Only staring Twiggy and Tommy Tune. His film productions include Lord of the Flies; Fahrenheit 451; Never Cry Wolf; and the Hoover mini-series, Portrait of a Marriage.

Bill Backer

Bill Backer grew up in Charleston, South Carolina. He attended Episcopal High School in Alexandria, Virginia. Following two years of service in the U.S. Navy, he entered Yale University where two musicals, he wrote before he graduated, received wide attention. Upon graduation, he entered the world of advertising and exhibited a talent for capturing America's mood in song. That ability propelled him to the top of the advertising business.

His musical commercials — some hit the American charts as songs — included *Here's to Good Friends, It's the Real Thing, If You've Got the Time, Hello Summertime*, and *Look that America. But, I'd Like to Teach the World to Sing* went to the top of the song charts world-wide. It helped to make Bill Backer — in the work of New York Times' *Advertising Age* — a "creative legend." In 1979, he co-founded what turned out to be the fastest growing agency in the history of advertising, Backer and Spielvogel, Inc., which soared to half a billion dollars in eleven years with America singing the ads using Bill Backer's ideas.

Backer retired from the ad-writing business in 1992, but he resides in The Plains, Virginia. His book, *The Care and Feeding of Ideas*, was published by Time Books in 1992. He has set music to *Playground*, a new musical comedy based on Grahame's *Wind in the Willows*.

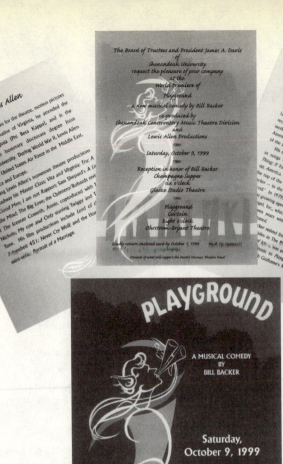

A MUSICAL COMEDY
BY
BILL BACKER

Saturday,
October 9, 1999

The Committee

Honorary Chairman

Mr. Lewis Allen

Committee Members

Mrs. Walter H. Aikens
Mrs. Dale M. Barley
Mrs. Murrell Bolliger
Mrs. J. Shep Campbell
Mrs. LeRoy Caudill
Mrs. Myron Dickerson
Mrs. H. Robert Edwards
Mrs. John D. Glover, Jr.
Mrs. T.C. Iden, Jr.
Ms Lore D. Michael
Mrs. Joyce Mull
Ms Jane D. Pittman
Mrs. James R. Ross
Ms Carolyn Rutherford
Ms Kitty Shendow
Mrs. J. Donald Shockey
Mrs. Richard Thomas
Ms Kami Williams
Mrs. Dan F. Wall
Mrs. C. Ridgely White, Jr.

PLAYGROUND

Music and Lyrics by Bill Backer

This world premiere, *Playground*, is co-produced by Shenandoah Conservatory Music Theatre Division and Lewis Allen Productions. It is a story of four friends who unite to try to save "a bit of paradise." They are, however, not ideally suited for the job. One is a self-indulgent toad given to bragging and boasting; another, a water rat, is a poet and a dreamer; a third, the gruff badger, is difficult and arbitrary, and the fourth, a coal miner's daughter doesn't really belong — at least not at first. How the four finally defeat the takeover specialist for Weasel and Welch, Inc., make for drama, both high and low. This is the world premiere of a brand new musical which, on the basis of its tuneful score, was selected by the Director's Company in New York for a preliminary staging last year. The score is by the author of such hits at *I'd Like to Teach the World to Sing, and Hello, Summertime.* This a show that seems to be Broadway-bound!

## Chapter 7

Speaking Up for Your Special Event

S peaking to groups about your organization, or company, and the event you are supporting may be the most difficult aspect of fund-raising for some, but in the end, it can be the most rewarding.

Line up speaking engagements to networking organizations for your fund-raising efforts. Networking groups are ones such as

- Chambers of Commerce
- Philanthropic organizations
- Women's and men's business organizations
- Churches
- Schools
- Colleges, business schools, and universities
- Professional organizations
- Neighborhood associations
- Hobbyists, such as bridge clubs

All of these are great sources of support and together constitute a major pipeline for getting the word out. You should ask the organizations you target for their mailing lists. Then invite the people on the list to a fund-raising event, such as a workshop.

Lining up a public speaking campaign is as easy as 1, 2, 3.

1. Format the sample letter (opposite page) to the organizations on your target contact list. Address the letter to the appropriate person, such as the president, meeting coordinator, or program chairman.

2. Mail the letter and follow up at least three days later via phone or personal visit. Be prepared. Have the details about the cause you're supporting and your date book handy for quick reference during your initial phone conversation. Try to line up a presentation immediately. Ask to meet personally with the contact to discuss your ideas further.

3. Send a presentation confirmation letter one week before the speaking engagement. Outline your presentation format and the items you will need to bring to the presentation. Doing so ensures that the presentation is allotted enough space and time.

A Gala Event!

Contacting Local Business Organizations

(Today's Date)
(President's Name*)
(Organization Name)
(Address)
(City, State, Zip)

Dear (President):

In an effort to increase our community involvement, (The Company Name), a (description of company or organization), is currently raising (funds, donations, specific item) for the (name of charity). As conscientious citizens, we are extremely sensitive to this cause.

(Description of charity, two paragraphs.)

(Efforts your group is taking to support this cause.)

When would it be convenient for me to address (organization) and make a presentation on this most important cause? As active members of the community, the (organization) will be interested in learning more about our efforts and how they too can participate.

My presentation will consist of the following: Welcome and introduction, slide presentation on the (charity), information on planned charity events for the local area, and how your organization can contribute to this cause.

Knowing your organization strongly believes in active involvement and "making a difference" in this community, I would like to assist you with meeting this objective.

I look forward to discussing this matter further with you. I will call in a few days to follow up.

Sincerely,

* This letter should be sent to any member of an organization who is a decision maker.

Public Speaking Presentation

- The presentation should be concise and informative. Tell the audience about your company or organization, talk about the charity you have chosen to support, and out-line fund-raising plans for the area. The presentation agenda should look something like the example on the next page.

- Stay focused on how your event affects the community. Ask for the participation of the group you're addressing. Tell them why you need their help and how their help will help somebody else.

- Begin with what you want them most to hear. Your lis-teners might not be able to stay until the end. To keep the audience's attention, keep it simple and keep it short.

- Show how the charity fits into the group's focus.

- Try to answer any possible objection in the body of your address, and then, if someone raises an objection during a question-and-answer period, gently remind the ques-tioner that the issue was mentioned in the speech: "As I said in my remarks..."

- Turn any negative questions into positive responses: "That's really a good question. Here's how the charity has affected me..." is a good answer.

Sample Presentation

2 minutes	Welcome and Introduction
3 minutes	Tell Your Organization's Story
	Briefly highlight the business or auxiliary.
3 minutes	Charity Presentation
	Highlight the program format and accomplishments (using material provided by the charity)
	Guest speaker (a representative of the charity)
5 minutes	Fund-raising Plan for Local Area
	Name events planned
	Set the bait for recruiting donations
	Hand out donation envelopes
5 minutes	Questions and Answers

A Gala Event!

Workshops and Seminars

Groups often feature programs on topics of interest to their members. A group of realtors, for instance, might be interested in hearing how maid service can help them. A closet-organizing expert might come in to give a speech. It's also possible to stage a seminar on a topic that will be of interest to the public as a way to generate excitement and donations. A seminar takes about 1.5 hours, and this is how it is organized:

5 minutes	Welcome and Introduction
5 minutes	Set Up the Seminar
	Tell the audience that they will do the following:
	Learn about your company/organization.
	Learn about [the topic of the seminar].
	Learn about organization of the charity.
10 minutes	Tell your company/organization story.
60 minutes	Offer useful information to the audience on the seminar topic.
5 minutes	Door prize giveaway

If you don't already have a seminar that can be used for a fund-raising tool, consider developing one. Or sponsor an outside speaker who would attract an audience. Many companies already have an expert who may be willing to attend your event, especially with the admission fee going toward a good cause.

A Gala Event!

OPERATION SMILE INTERNATIONAL

and

Saks Fifth Avenue

INVITE YOU TO JOIN US FOR

AN EVENING ON FIFTH AVENUE

At

SAKS FIFTH AVENUE
5555 WISCONSIN AVENUE
CHEVY CHASE, MARYLAND

MAY 16, 1992
7:30 P.M.

COCKTAILS
BUFFET DINNER
DANCING

SILENT AND LIVE AUCTIONS

CREATIVE BLACK TIE   RSVP BY MAY 6, 1992

$75 PER PERSON

Please use Mall Entrance

Evening on Fifth Avenue

## Chapter 8

Finding Sponsors

If you are having a huge function or event, a great way to underwrite costs is to have sponsorships from local businesses and individuals. Look through the event checklist of items you will need for the event and find sponsors who can provide such large items as

- Site location rental
- Catering
- Entertainment
- Invitation printing
- Party favors
- Auction item
- Prize drawing

A sure-fire way to obtain sponsorships is to have as many business leaders involved with the charity function as possible. People love to donate their products and/or services for local events—donating improves their image in the community.

For example, hotels will often let a charitable cause use a room free or at a discount. Not having to rent space frees up resources for other expenses. Printers, caterers, and other service providers can write off a portion, if not all, of the expense on their taxes. The event's donations committee should help solicit sponsors for each part of the function.

Acknowledging sponsors is an important follow-through to any successful charity event. There are three ways to do this:

- List them on the event program.
- Mention them in the press releases, especially the "post" press release.
- If the event has one major sponsor or a few principal ones, acknowledge them in the announcements at the event.

If you have not planned to print an event program, consider printing just a listing of sponsors that can be distributed at the function. A list of sponsors is an economical alternative; however, if you are planning a formal event, a program is recommended. Placement of acknowledgments in the program is shown in the sample in the "Invitations" chapter that follows.

## Chapter 9

Invitations & Programs

You get only one chance to make a good first impression—and the invitation sets the tone for the event. The paper stock you select, the typeface you choose, and the layout of the elements on the page join with the specifics about what, when, and where to give the recipient a good idea whether the event will be casual or formal, lively or stately. For example, for an evening of jazz, you wouldn't send out invitations in the fancy script used for formal weddings.

Your Invitation Should Fit the Occasion

Being invited to a party is fun! Your invitations should get people excited about coming to the event from the moment they open the envelope. You might have someone on the committee who is a graphic artist who can help design the invitation and program. But have it professionally done. You'll save time and expense in the long run.

The invitation & program chair selects a designer for the invitation and program. The chairperson also arranges for printing the invitation, program, and any other printed material. The entire event team should approve the final invitation copy and design. The invitation & program chair ideally should bring a design layout—a sample of what the invitation will actually look like—to the full committee meeting so that people will see exactly what it looks like. If a computer-generated or hand-drawn sample isn't feasible, the chair can at least bring samples of the paper and typeface.

Designing Elements

- Consider choosing one of the many preprinted papers available in stationary stores in various sizes.

- Most printers can be very helpful in advising you about the mood that different typefaces engender.

- Often printers will help you select a layout as well.

- The look of the invitations may be carried through to the program to lend your material continuity and style.

- Pertinent information on the invitation includes what type of event it is; when, where, and what time the event will be held; prices or suggested donations.

- Include a postage-paid response envelope and a response card for a significantly higher RSVP and contribution rate. Consider including a donation check-off on the response card, making it convenient for people to contribute, even if they can't attend the event.

- On programs, it's important to make sure all the sponsors that want to be recognized are included and that their names are spelled correctly.

- The entire event team should look over the material before it is printed to make sure everything is included and that there are no errors!

- Ask the printer to donate his services in return for acknowledgment in the program. And don't forget to give the printer a complimentary pair of tickets to the event.

- Take a complete invitation to the post office to make sure you'll have the right amount of postage on each.

- One way that your company can maximize its contact is by printing a list of short facts about the company or cause on a detachable flap on the donation envelope.

- Mail the invitations early. If you are conducting a year-long campaign, mail them two months ahead of time. Otherwise, count on three to four weeks. People lead such busy lives you want to make sure you get on their social calendars!

Addressing Invitations

Invitations should be addressed as carefully as those for a wedding. You'll need a committee to help, each member of which should have excellent handwriting and be attentive to detail. Here are the rules for formal invitations:

- Spell out symbols (such as "and" instead of an ampersand).

- Write out the full name.

- The only abbreviations allowed are Dr., Mr., Mrs., Ms., and Jr.

- No middle initials are allowed; spell out the name. If you don't know what the initial stands for, omit it.

- Never write "and family."

- Write out "East," "West," "North," and "South."

- Only house numbers and the ZIP code may be written as numerals; spell out everything as a word ("Twenty-fifth Avenue" instead of "25th Avenue").

- Write out "Avenue" and similar words (such as "Road" and "Street").

- Spell out the state names.
- Use permanent black ink.

 **Tip**

Every invitation or program must include:
— Type of event
— Date
— Location
— Time
— Ticket prices and/or suggested donation

 **Tip**

Felt tip pens with medium or wide points are best for hand addressing invitations and are easier to read on name tags than ball point pens.

After the Invitations Are Mailed

The telephone solicitation committee follows up written invitations to key invitees with a phone call. This committee should be large enough so that no one is overburdened with too many calls to make.

The chair of the telephone solicitation committee must coordinate the follow-up calls with the mailing list chair. It wouldn't do to have calls going out before invitations had a chance to arrive.

- Give committee members a list of names and numbers, along with a phone script (p. 106).
- The mailing list may be categorized into A, B, and C donors depending on the potential size of their donation if the list is very large.

 **Tip**

Key invitees must be called to make sure they have all the event details straight—such as when and where the event will be.

- Key invitees should be called shortly after the invitations are dropped off at the post office. Ideally, committee members who personally know those likely to be generous donors should make the follow-up calls. Calling makes sure these people have all the event details straight. Personal calls also emphasize how important these people are to the endeavor.

- Keep the calls cordial and brief.

A Gala Event!

Sample Phone Script

Invitation Follow-up

Henry: "Hello, may I speak with Mr. Smith please?"

"Mr. Smith, my name is Henry Higgins, and I am with Hats on Every Head. I am calling to follow up on the Park Beautification Program invitation you recently received? Do you plan on attending?"

(For positive response)

Mr. Smith: Yes.

Henry: "That's wonderful, Mr. Smith. I'm sure you agree that this is a worthwhile cause, and I look forward to meeting you. I will be looking for your RSVP card in the mail. If you know of anyone else who would be interested in participating or making a contribution, please have them contact me at (333) 333-3333. Goodbye."

(For negative response)

Mr. Smith: No.

Henry: "Well, it's a shame that you won't be able to attend our charity event. Would there be anyone else in your family or company that you might send on your behalf?" (Response may be yes or no.)

(If yes)

Mr. Smith: Yes.

Henry: "That's wonderful. I will look for your RSVP with their names. It's a shame you won't be able to join us, but please keep our event in mind for next year. Goodbye."

(If no)

Mr. Smith: No.

Henry: "If you should change your mind or know of anyone who would care to participate, please call me at (333) 333-3333. I appreciate your taking the time to talk with me; please keep our event in mind for next year! Goodbye."

Sample Invitation

Simple Simon Pie Company

cordially invites you to attend

The Leader Dogs for the Blind

Black Tie Dinner

To be held at the Holly Hills Wood Hotel

6000 North Hudson Place

Washington, Virginia

Grand Ballroom

The Third of May

RSVP by (date)   Reception 6:00 p.m.

Black tie   Dinner 7:00 p.m.

Sample RSVP Card

Simple Simon Pie Company / Leader Dogs for the Blind

(return address)

Yes—I would like to attend the Leader Dogs for the Blind Black Tie Dinner

_____ Please reserve _____ tables of 10 at $1,000 per table.

_____ Please reserve _____ places at $100 per person.

_____ Enclosed is a check in the amount of $ _____ .

Sorry—I cannot attend the dinner; however, I still wish to make a contribution in recognition of the charity in the amount of $ _____ .

Name _____

Address _____

Phone (Business) _____ (Home) _____

Checks should be made payable to the Leader Dogs for the Blind and are tax-deductible to the extent of the law.

Please list the names of guests covered by this reservation on the reverse side.

RSVP Card Back

Attendee Names

_____

_____

_____

_____

_____

_____

_____

_____

_____

_____

_____

_____

_____

Sample Event Program

Cover

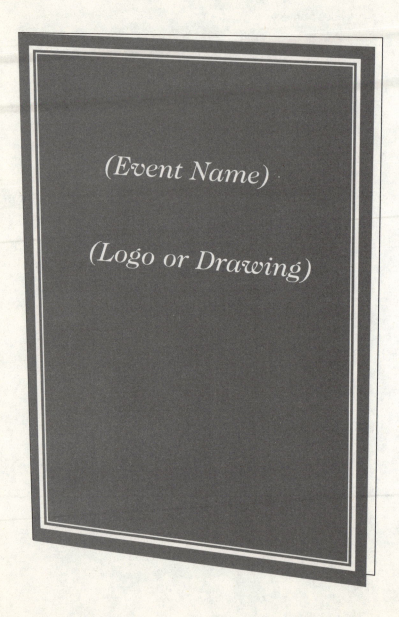

Sample Event Program *(continued)*

Inside Cover

Dinner Menu

_____

_____

_____

_____

_____

_____

_____

_____

_____

Food Provided by ABC Catering

Entertainment Provided by XYZ Music

Sample Event Program *(continued)*

Inside Back Cover

Program

Welcome & Introductions

(Charity Chairperson's Name)

Dinner

(Spokesperson's Name/Presentation)

∽   ∽

Silent Auction

Dancing

Sample Event Program *(continued)*

Back Outside Cover

Honorary Chairperson
(if you have one)

Charity Committee

_____ _____

_____ _____

_____ _____

Sponsors

_____ _____

_____ _____

Printing Courtesy of (donating printer)

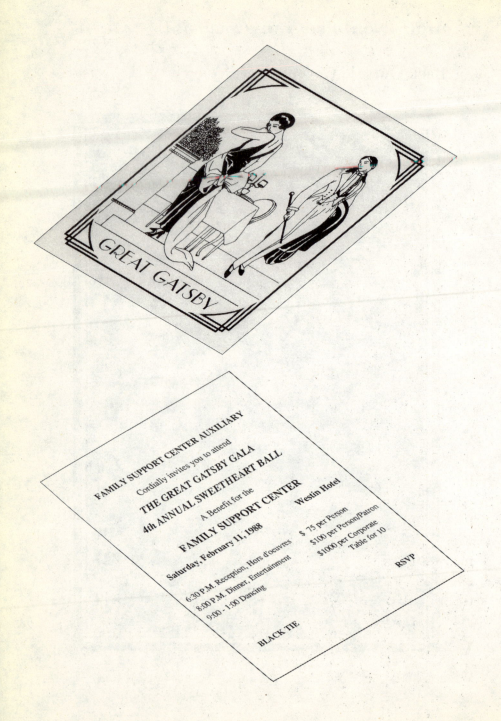

GREAT GATSBY

FAMILY SUPPORT CENTER AUXILIARY

Cordially invites you to attend

THE GREAT GATSBY GALA
4th ANNUAL SWEETHEART BALL

A Benefit for the

FAMILY SUPPORT CENTER

Westin Hotel

Saturday, February 11, 1988

$ 75 per Person
$100 per Person/Patron
$1000 per Corporate
Table for 10

6:30 P.M. Reception, Hors d'oeuvres
8:00 P.M. Dinner, Entertainment
9:00 - 1:00 Dancing

RSVP

BLACK TIE

## Chapter 10

After the Event

I n the month after the event or charity campaign—once you've had a little time to relax after all the work you've done and overseen—it's time to take care of the final details.

First, it's very important to send thank-you notes to everyone who helped you and the committees make the event a success. You couldn't have accomplished it without the participants or the donors. You must let them know that you appreciate them—and look forward to their contribution next year.

A key to building on the success you had with this event is to critique all the activities that were connected with it. Discuss what went well and what didn't go so well with everything leading up to the event and at the event itself. Even if you met or exceeded the goal, you should be figuring out what can be done to polish and improve the event next year.

Wrap-up Meeting

When you invite each chair of the Event Team to the meeting, ask him or her to bring a written report for the files. This report should include the following:

- Committee membership
- Responsibilities of the committee and each member
- Description of projects, how much they cost, who was responsible for them
- Analysis of chairperson
- Suggestions for the future

Attached to each report should be the chairperson's notebook containing notes, copies of contracts and invoices, and samples of completed projects where appropriate (invitations, programs, news releases, and so forth).

At the meeting

- Ask each chair to summarize his or her report.
- Ask for additional comments from everyone on the committee.
- Think about all the aspects of the event and brainstorm ways to make each part stronger. No ideas are bad. Really, no negative comment is bad, because you can always use it for next year's event.
- Collect all the reports and file them in a binder for next year.
- If you are supporting a charity, encourage the committee members to talk about the charity and the event within the community during the year to "keep it alive." If a community knows to expect this activity as an annual event, people will look for the invitations and place it on their social calendars. Soon it will be general knowledge what charity the company or organization supports.
- Set a date for the next charity event for the following year. Remember—you can never begin too early!

Tip

Written reports from each committee chair are an invaluable resource for the future. With this kind of history at the committee's fingertips, they won't have to reinvent the wheel next year—instead, you can build on this year's success.

Examples of Charity Thank-You Notes

Dear Event Sponsor,

I am writing on behalf of the (XYZ Company) to thank you for your generous donation of (item) to the (event name). You truly helped make this event a success! The moneys raised at the (event) will (help in some specific way).

We are pleased to announce that with your assistance we were able to reach our goal of $_____ and hope to top that with our 2nd Annual Event.

Again, thank you for your sponsorship. If you would be interested in participating next year on the Event Team, please don't hesitate to contact me.

Sincerely,

Examples of Charity Thank-You Notes
(continued)

Dear $ Donor,

I am writing on behalf of (XYZ Company) to thank you for your generous donation to the worthwhile cause (name of charity). You truly helped make this event a success! The moneys raised will assist (someone in some specific way).

We are pleased to announce that with your assistance we were able to reach our goal of $_____ and hope to top that with our 2nd Annual Event.

Again, thank you for your generous donation. If you would be interested in participating next year on the Event Team, please don't hesitate to contact me.

Sincerely,

Dear Event Team Member,

Thank you for making the (name of event) a success! It is rewarding to write this note, knowing that together we have made a difference! I look forward to begin work on next year's event and hope to have you on the team!

Keep in touch.

Sincerely,

Final Thought

I hope you have as much fun planning your "gala" as I did in writing this book. All my suggestions are for one purpose: To help you achieve the goals of your special event. Events should be fun, not ordeals. It is my wish that if you follow all my checklists and tips, you can't fail.

Happy Event Planning!

A Gala Event!